TRANSNATIONAL TERRORISM: CONVENTIONS AND COMMENTARY

A COMPILATION OF TREATIES, AGREEMENTS AND DECLARATIONS OF ESPECIAL INTEREST TO THE UNITED STATES

RICHARD B. LILLICH
Howard W. Smith Professor of Law
University of Virginia School of Law
Editor

CONTENTS

ACKNOWLEDGMENTS

This book had its origins in two reports — *Multinational Conventions and Agreements Relating to the Punishment of Terrorist Acts* and *Future International Efforts to Ensure the Prosecution and Punishment of Acts of International Terrorism: The Use of Treaties* — prepared by the editor for the Office of the Legal Adviser of the U.S. Department of State in September and December 1976 under contract No. 1724-62-225 with the Procedural Aspects of International Law Institute to study "Sanctuary and Safe-Haven for Terrorists: The Relevancy of International Law."

This greatly revised and updated version of the above reports, prepared with the assistance of Messrs. Kenneth R. Lee, Ross Clayton Mulford and Clayton Robert Barker III, students at the University of Virginia School of Law, is designed to make the essential material contained herein conveniently available to the general public. For the record, it is the work product of the editor and not the Institute or the Department of State, both of which have cooperated generously in its preparation but naturally are not responsible for any errors of judgment or detail.

INTRODUCTION

Although it took the Hostage Crisis to bring it home to the United States public, transnational terrorism [1] is not a recent phenomenon. From the French Reign of Terror through the activities of various anarchist groups in the late 19th and early 20th centuries to the numerous operations staged by the Popular Front for the Liberation of Palestine over the past decade, both States and their opponents have employed calculated acts of violence in their attempts to achieve political objectives. What is new, as a relatively recent CIA study makes clear, is the spillover of terrorist activity onto the international scene. "Advances in technology and growing world interdependence have afforded terrorists new mobility, new targets, new

---

1. No attempt will be made to define the term "terrorism" for purposes of this volume. As the late Judge Baxter aptly observed, "[w]e have cause to regret that a legal concept of 'terrorism' was ever inflicted upon us. The term is imprecise; it is ambiguous; and above all, it serves no operative legal purpose." Baxter, *A Skeptical Look at the Concept of Terrorism*, 7 AKRON L. REV. 380, 380 (1974). Moreover, to paraphrase Justice Stewart, one may not be able to define it, but one knows it when one sees it. Jacobellis v. Ohio, 378 U.S. 184, 197 (1964) (concurring opinion). The term therefore is used for linguistic convenience to cover a host of acts made criminal by the national law of most States, as well as certain acts — such as aerial hijacking — specifically made criminal by international agreements.

The adjective "transnational" is used to denote terrorism with one or more international components, such as "incidents in which terrorists go abroad to strike their targets, select victims or targets because of their connection to a foreign state . . ., attack airlines on international flights, or force airliner to fly to another country." Jenkins, International Terrorism: A New Mode of Conflict 9 (California Seminar on Arms Control and Foreign Policy, Research Paper No. 48, 1975). It does not cover "the local activities of dissident groups when carried out against a local government or citizens in their own country if no foreign connection is involved." *Id.*

weaponry, and the near certain prospect that their more dramatic acts will receive prompt and world-wide publicity," the study concludes. "Moreover, recent changes in the overall political and economic climate have provided terrorists with a somewhat more hospitable environment in which to operate." [2]

Modern society, additionally, is especially vulnerable to terrorist activities. John Karkashian, then Acting Director of the Department of State's Office for Combating Terrorism, told the Senate Foreign Relations Committee in 1977 that "[b]etween January 1968 and December 1976 there were approximately 1,150 separate international terrorist incidents. While the progression has not been even, the overall trend in the annual totals of these incidents is increasing. Nineteen hundred and seventy-six saw a record of 239 separate incidents." [3] This has borne out his gloomy prophesy: in the first eight months of 1980 alone over 500 incidents had been recorded. [4]

The reasons for this upsurge in transnational terrorism, according to Karkashian, include the following: (1) the political fragmentation taking place around the world; (2) the grievances, real or imagined, that disaffected national groups have against various States; (3) the availability of modern weapons which enhances the striking power of small groups; (4) the fact that commercial aircraft provide not only readymade hostages, but also a place to confine

---

2. CIA, RESEARCH STUDY, INTERNATIONAL AND TRANSNATIONAL TERRORISM: DIAGNOSIS AND PROGNOSIS 7 (April 1976).

3. *Hearings on International Terrorism Before the Subcomm. on Foreign Assistance of the Senate Comm. on Foreign Relations,* 95th Cong., 1st Sess. 31 (1977) (testimony of John K. Karkashian, Acting Director, Officer for Conbating Terrorism, Department of State).

4. BUREAU OF PUBLIC AFFAIRS, U.S. DEP'T OF STATE, CURRENT POLICY No. 230, THE CHALLENGE OF TERRORISM: THE 1980's, at 1 (address by Hon. Anthony Quainton, Director of the Office for Combating Terrorism, Sept. 25, 1970).

them and the means to transport them and their captors
anywhere in the world; (5) the financing, arming and
training of terrorists by various States, which also give
them sanctuary and safe-haven after their operations; and
(6) the worldwide media coverage which surrounds major
terrorist incidents, thus assuring terrorists of worldwide
attention for their cause.

Given the extent of the threat, one must agree with the
CIA study that "the international response to terrorism has
been relatively weak and ineffective." [5] Initially, as Brian
Jenkins of the Rand Corporation has pointed out, both
tranditional "[i]nternational law and the rules of warfare as
they now exist are inadequate to cope with this new mode
of conflict." [6] Efforts to legislate new solutions have pro-
duced three international conventions covering aerial
hijackings: the 1963 Tokyo Convention on Offenses
Committed on Board Aircraft, ratified by 107 States; the
1970 Hague Convention for the Suppression of the
Unlawful Seizure of Aircraft, ratified by 113 States; and the
1971 Montreal Convention for the Suppression of Unlawful
Acts Against the Safety of Civil Aviation, ratified by 111
States. The last two of these conventions requires States
Parties to make such offenses subject to severe penalties
and to prosecute or extradite offenders.

The conventions, however, do not constitute a truly effective constraint even on hijacking. In the first place,
one-third of the United Nations' membership — including
a good many States who either support or give sanctuary
and safe-haven to terrorists — are not parties to them. Secondly, the prosecute-or-extradite obligation has been
deemed subject to international law's traditional political
offense exception, a doctrine originally designed to afford

---

5. CIA, RESEARCH STUDY, *supra* note 2, at 26.
6. Jenkins, *supra* note 1, at 16.

political asylum to opponents of repressive regimes, but one which too often in recent years has served as an escape clause for States anxious or willing to protect terrorists. Finally, the conventions fail to provide for the application of sanctions against States which, while parties to them, simply refuse to comply at all.

Following the Munich massacre in 1972, the United States submitted a draft convention to the United Nations aimed at limiting the "export" of terrorism, but this effort was blunted in the General Assembly and eventually buried under a proposed study of the underlying causes of terrorism. However, the following year the General Assembly did adopt the Convention on the Prevention and Punishment of Crimes Against Internationally Protected Persons, modeled after the Hague and Montreal Conventions, which contains a prosecute-or-extradite provision. This treaty, which came into force in 1977 and has been ratified so far by 54 States, is not the comprehensive convention favored by some legal experts, but its "piecemeal" approach may offer a more promising alternative solution. Indeed, the United Nations followed up this approach in 1979 by adopting an International Convention Against the Taking of Hostages. Since approximately one-third of all incidents of transnational terrorism involve the taking of hostages — diplomats, corporate executives, tourists, and innocent bystanders — such a convention, when it comes into force, will be a significant step forward in developing a legal regime in this area. Other conventions in other areas can be expected during the 1980's if States follow through on this "piecemeal" approach to combating terrorism.

The conventions mentioned above, along with other international agreements proscribing transnational terrorist acts, are gathered together here for the first time in one convenient volume. Part I contains the 13 major multilateral conventions and agreements in the field. After a brief Editor's Note, the complete text or the relevant articles of each instrument is set out, followed by a complete list of the States Parties, their declarations and reservations, United States action with respect to the agreement, and citations to any relevant United States cases. This part, the major portion of the volume, thus provides the reader with a complete overview of the conventional international law norms governing transnational terrorism.[7]

As stated above, the prosecute-or-extradite obligation contained in most of these recent agreements is a particularly effective technique for enforcing such norms. In addition to bilateral extradition treaties which frequently come into play, many States also are parties to multilateral extradition treaties and agreements. These multilateral extradition instruments generally contain provisions specifically excluding political offenses from the extradition process.[8] A fugitive terrorist who claims that his acts were politically motivated, as is often the case, raises particularly difficult issues as to whether the offense of which he is accused is a political one or not. With respect to these

---

7. For a discussion of the customary international law norms governing transnational terrorism, see Lillich & Paxman, *State Responsibility for Injuries to Aliens Occasioned by Terrorists Activities,* 26 AM. U.L. REV. 217 (1977).

8. Exceptions to the exceptions often are created by so-called *Belgian* clauses, which exclude certain terrorist acts, *e.g.,* assassinations of a Head of State, from the category of political offenses. *See Measure to Prevent International Terrorism Which Endangers or Takes Innocent Human Lives or Jeopardizes Fundamental Freedoms, and Study of the Underlying Causes of Those Forms of Terrorism and Acts of Violence Which Lie in Misery, Frustrations, Grievance and Despair and Which Cause Some People to Sacrifice Human Lives Including Their Own, in an Attempt to Effect Radical Changes,* U.N. DOC. A/C.6/418, at 17 (1972).

multilateral extradition agreements, summaries of which are contained in Part II of the volume along with the same relevant material that follows the Part I agreements, the volume seeks to identify the category of extraditable offenses, provisions on political offenses, and any exclusions from the category of political offenses.

Some years ago the close relationship between the law and practice of asylum and the punishment of terrorists was starkly illustrated by a study of the enforcement responses by States to aircraft hijackers.[9] In the case of those hijackings which did not terminate in the same State where they were initiated, it was discovered that 70 percent of the cases resulted in the grant of asylum to the hijackers. Fugitive terrorists claiming that they are political refugees naturally seek asylum in sympathetic States. The question then arises whether they have the right to seek and enjoy asylum and, especially, whether those agreements governing asylum create any conflicting obligations upon States that may require them to derogate from their prosecute-or-extradite obligations under the agreements found in Part I. Thus Part III of the volume contains summaries of the existing agreements that relate to asylum, plus the same relevant material that follows the Part I agreements.

The volume contains three appendices. The first contains, for the record, the 1937 League of Nations Convention for the Prevention and Punishment of Terrorism and the 1972 draft convention which the United States submitted to the United Nations. The second contains, for informational purposes, proposed conventions drafted by the International Law Association, the Procedural Aspects of International Law Institute, and the American Bar Association. The third, supplementing the lists of States Parties found after

---

9. N. Joyner, Aerial Hijacking as an International Crime 186 (1974).

all the agreements contained in Parts I to III, contains an alphabetical, country-by-country list of ratifications and accessions to all the agreements found in the volume. This appendix enables the reader to determine easily what obligations a particular State may have with respect to a particular terrorist situation and, secondly, what States are in a legal position to demand extradition of the alleged offender if that State elects not to prosecute him.

The information flow in this volume stops as of 1 March 1982. Regular supplements will keep the volume up-to-date.

KEY TO ABBREVIATIONS

Hudson: M. Hudson, *International Legislation* (1941).
Malloy: W. Malloy, *Treaties, Conventions, International Acts, Protocols and Agreements* (1910).

I. CONVENTIONS PROSCRIBING TERRORIST ACTS

A. *General*

1. Convention on Offenses and Certain Other Acts Committed on Board Aircraft (Tokyo Convention), *signed* Sept. 14, 1963, *entered into force* Dec. 4, 1969, 20 U.S.T. 2941, T.I.A.S. No. 6768, 704 U.N.T.S. 219 (*entered into force* for U.S. Dec. 4, 1969).

Editor's Note

The Tokyo Convention applies to offenses against penal laws and to acts, whether or not they are offenses, which may or do jeopardize the safety of the aircraft or of persons or property therein, or which jeopardize good order and discipline on board the aircraft while it is in flight, on the surface of the high seas, or in an area outside the territory of any State (Article 1).

While the Convention is concerned with ensuring that at least one State has jurisdiction of the alleged offender, it contains only limited provisions for the trial of persons accused of offenses under it. Article 3 provides that the State of registration of the aircraft is competent to exercise jurisdiction over the alleged offender and, further, that each Contracting State is obliged to take necessary measures to establish its jurisdiction as the State of registration. Even though a Contracting State is required to adopt the laws necessary to give its courts jurisdiction, it is not obliged to ensure that all alleged offenders will be prosecuted (Article 13).

The Convention provides for a Contracting State to take delivery from the aircraft commander of a suspected offender (Article 13), but it places no obligation on the receiving State to grant extradition of a suspected offender to a State that has jurisdiction to try him (Article 16). Offenses committed on aircraft registered in a Contracting State are merely to be treated, for the purposes of extradition, as if they had been committed not only in the place in which they had occurred, but also in the territory of the State of registration of the aircraft (Article 16).

Text of the Convention

CHAPTER I—SCOPE OF THE CONVENTION

ARTICLE 1

1. This Convention shall apply in respect of:
   (a) offences against penal law;
   (b) acts which, whether or not they are offences, may or do jeopardize the safety of the aircraft or of persons or property therein or which jeopardize good order and discipline on board.
2. Except as provided in Chapter III, this Convention shall apply in respect of offences committed or acts done by a person on board any aircraft registered in a Contracting State, while that aircraft is in flight or on the surface of the high seas or of any other area outside the territory of any state.
3. For the purposes of this Convention, an aircraft is considered to be in flight from the moment when power is applied for the purpose of take-off until the moment when the landing run ends.
4. This Convention shall not apply to aircraft used in military, customs or police services.

2

ARTICLE 2

Without prejudice to the provisions of Article 4 and except when the safety of the aircraft or of persons or property on board so requires, no provision of this Convention shall be interpreted as authorizing or requiring any action in respect of offences against penal laws of a political nature or those based on racial or religious discrimination.

CHAPTER II—JURISDICTION

ARTICLE 3

1. The state of registration of the aircraft is competent to exercise jurisdiction over offences and acts committed on board.

2. Each Contracting State shall take such measures as may be necessary to establish its jurisdiction as the state of registration over offences committed on board aircraft registered in such state.

3. This Convention does not exclude any criminal jurisdiction exercised in accordance with national law.

ARTICLE 4

A Contracting State which is not the state of registration may not interfere with an aircraft in flight in order to exercise its criminal jurisdiction over an offence committed on board except in the following cases:

(a) the offence has effect on the territory of such state;

(b) the offence has been committed by or against a national or permanent resident of such state;

(c) the offence is against the security of such state;

(d) the offence consists of a breach of any rules or regulations relating to the flight or manoeuvre of aircraft in force in such state;

3

(e) the exercise of jurisdiction is necessary to ensure the observance of any obligation of such state under a multilateral international agreement.

Chapter III—Powers of the Aircraft Commander

Article 5

1. The provisions of this chapter shall not apply to offences and acts committed or about to be committed by a person on board an aircraft in flight in the airspace of the state of registration or over the high seas or any other area outside the territory of any state unless the last point of take-off or the next point of intended landing is situated in a state other than that of registration, or the aircraft subsequently flies in the airspace of a state other than that of registration with such person still on board.

2. Notwithstanding the provisions of Article 1, paragraph 3, an aircraft shall, for the purposes of this chapter, be considered to be in flight at any time from the moment when all its external doors are closed following embarkation until the moment when any such door is opened for disembarkation. In the case of a forced landing, the provisions of this chapter shall continue to apply with respect to offences and acts committed on board until competent authorities of a state take over the responsibility for the aircraft and for the persons and property on board.

Article 6

1. The aircraft commander may, when he has reasonable grounds to believe that a person has committed, or is about to commit, on board the aircraft, an offence or act contemplated in Article 1, paragraph 1, impose upon such person reasonable measures including restraint which are necessary:

4

(a) to protect the safety of the aircraft, or of persons or property therein; or

(b) to maintain good order and discipline on board; or

(c) to enable him to deliver such person to competent authorities or to disembark him in accordance with the provisions of this chapter.

2. The aircraft commander may require or authorize the assistance of other crew members and may request or authorize, but not require, the assistance of passengers to restrain any person whom he is entitled to restrain. Any crew member or passenger may also take reasonable preventive measures without such authorization when he has reasonable grounds to believe that such action is immediately necessary to protect the safety of the aircraft, or of persons or property therein.

Article 7

Measures of restraint imposed upon a person in accordance with Article 6 shall not be continued beyond any point at which the aircraft lands unless:

(a) such point is in the territory of a non-Contracting State and its authorities refuse to permit disembarkation of that person or those measures have been imposed in accordance with Article 6, paragraph (1)(c) in order to enable his delivery to competent authorities;

(b) the aircraft makes a forced landing and the aircraft commander is unable to deliver that person to competent authorities; or

(c) that person agrees to onward carriage under restraint.

2. The aircraft commander shall as soon as practicable, and if possible before landing in the territory of a state with a person on board who has been placed under restraint in

accordance with the provisions of Article 6, notify the authorities of such state of the fact that a person on board is under restraint and of the reasons for such restraint.

ARTICLE 8

1. The aircraft commander may, in so far as it is necessary for the purpose of subparagraph (a) or (b) of paragraph 1 of Article 6, disembark in the territory of any state in which the aircraft lands any person who he has reasonable grounds to believe has committed, or is about to commit, on board the aircraft an act contemplated in Article 1, paragraph 1(b).

2. The aircraft commander shall report to the authorities of the state in which he disembarks any person pursuant to this article, the fact of, and the reasons for, such disembarkation.

ARTICLE 9

1. The aircraft commander may deliver to the competent authorities of any Contracting State in the territory of which the aircraft lands any person who he has reasonable grounds to believe has committed on board the aircraft an act which, in his opinion, is a serious offence according to the penal law of the state of registration of the aircraft.

2. The aircraft commander shall as soon as practicable and if possible before landing in the territory of a Contracting State with a person on board whom the aircraft commander intends to deliver in accordance with the preceding paragraph, notify the authorities of such state of his intention to deliver such person and the reasons therefor.

3. The aircraft commander shall furnish the authorities to whom any suspected offender is delivered in accordance

6

with the provisions of this article with evidence and information which, under the law of the state of registration of the aircraft, are lawfully in his possession.

ARTICLE 10

For actions taken in accordance with this Convention, neither the aircraft commander, any other member of the crew, any passenger, the owner or operator of the aircraft, nor the person on whose behalf the flight was performed shall be held responsible in any proceeding on account of the treatment undergone by the person against whom the actions were taken.

CHAPTER IV—UNLAWFUL SEIZURE OF AIRCRAFT

ARTICLE 11

1. When a person on board has unlawfully committed by force or threat thereof an act of interference, seizure, or other wrongful exercise of control of an aircraft in flight or when such an act is about to be committed, Contracting States shall take all appropriate measures to restore control of the aircraft to its lawful commander or to preserve his control of the aircraft.

2. In the cases contemplated in the preceding paragraph, the Contracting State in which the aircraft lands shall permit its passengers and crew to continue their journey as soon as practicable, and shall return the aircraft and its cargo to the persons lawfully entitled to possession.

Chapter V—Powers and Duties of States

Article 12

Any Contracting State shall allow the commander of an aircraft registered in another Contracting State to disembark any person pursuant to Article 8, paragraph 1.

Article 13

1. Any Contracting State shall take delivery of any person whom the aircraft commander delivers pursuant to Article 9, paragraph 1.

2. Upon being satisfied that the circumstances so warrant, any Contracting State shall take custody or other measures to ensure the presence of any person suspected of an act contemplated in Article 11, paragraph 1, and of any person of whom it has taken delivery. The custody and other measures shall be as provided in the law of that state but may only be continued for such time as is reasonably necessary to enable any criminal or extradition proceedings to be instituted.

3. Any person in custody pursuant to the previous paragraph shall be assisted in communicating immediately with the nearest appropriate representative of the state of which he is a national.

4. Any Contracting State, to which a person is delivered pursuant to Article 9, paragraph 1, or in whose territory an aircraft lands following the commission of an act contemplated in Article 11, paragraph 1, shall immediately make a preliminary enquiry into the facts.

5. When a state, pursuant to this article, has taken a person into custody, it shall immediately notify the state of registration of the aircraft and the state of nationality of the detained person and, if it considers it advisable, any other

8

interested state of the fact that such person is in custody and of the circumstances which warrant his detention. The state which makes the preliminary enquiry contemplated in paragraph 4 of this article shall promptly report its findings to the said states and shall indicate whether it intends to exercise jurisdiction.

ARTICLE 14

1. When any person has been disembarked in accordance with Article 8, paragraph 1, or delivered in accordance with Article 9, paragraph 1, or has disembarked after committing an act contemplated in Article 11, paragraph 1, and when such person cannot or does not desire to continue his journey and the state of landing refuses to admit him, that state may, if the person in question is not a national or permanent resident of that state, return him to the territory of the state of which he is a national or permanent resident or to the territory of the state in which he began his journey by air.

2. Neither disembarkation, nor delivery, nor the taking of custody or other measures contemplated in Article 13, paragraph 2, nor return of the person concerned, shall be considered as admission to the territory of the Contracting State concerned for the purpose of its law relating to entry or admission of persons and nothing in this Convention shall affect the law of a Contracting State relating to the explusion of persons from its territory.

ARTICLE 15

1. Without prejudice to Article 14, any person who has been disembarked in accordance with Article 8, paragraph 1, or delivered in accordance with Article 9, paragraph 1, or has disembarked after committing an act contemplated in

Article 11, paragraph 1, and who desires to continue his journey shall be at liberty as soon as practicable to proceed to any destination of his choice unless his presence is required by the law of the state of landing for the purpose of extradition or criminal proceedings.

2. Without prejudice to its law as to entry and admission to, and extradition and expulsion from its territory, a Contracting State in whose territory a person has been disembarked in accordance with Article 8, paragraph 1, or delivered in accordance with Article 9, paragraph 1 or has disembarked and is suspected of having committed an act contemplated in Article 11, paragraph 1, shall accord to such person treatment which is no less favourable for his protection and security than that accorded to nationals of such Contracting State in like circumstances.

CHAPTER VI—OTHER PROVISIONS

ARTICLE 16

1. Offences committed on aircraft registered in a Contracting State shall be treated, for the purpose of extradition, as if they had been committed not only in the place in which they have occurred but also in the territory of the state of registration of the aircraft.

2. Without prejudice to the provisions of the preceding paragraph, nothing in this Convention shall be deemed to create an obligation to grant extradition.

ARTICLE 17

In taking any measures for investigation or arrest or otherwise exercising jurisdiction in connection with any offence committed on board an aircraft the Contracting States shall pay due regard to the safety and other interests of air navigation and shall so act as to avoid unnecessary delay of the aircraft, passengers, crew or cargo.

ARTICLE 18

If Contracting States establish joint air transport operating organizations or international operating agencies, which operate aircraft not registered in any one state, those states shall, according to the circumstances of the case, designate the state among them which, for the purposes of this Convention, shall be considered as the state of registration and shall give notice thereof to the International Civil Aviation Organization which shall communicate the notice to all states parties to this Convention.

CHAPTER VII—FINAL CLAUSES

ARTICLE 19

Until the date on which this Convention comes into force in accordance with the provisions of Article 21, it shall remain open for signature on behalf of any state which at that date is a Member of the United Nations or of any of the Specialized Agencies.

ARTICLE 20

1. This Convention shall be subject to ratification by the signatory states in accordance with their constitutional procedures.

2. The instruments of ratification shall be deposited with the International Civil Aviation Organization.

ARTICLE 21

1. As soon as twelve of the signatory states have deposited their instruments of ratification of this Convention, it shall come into force between them on the ninetieth day after the date of the deposit of the twelfth instrument of ratification. It shall come into force for each state ratifying thereafter on the ninetieth day after the deposit of its instrument of ratification.

2. As soon as this Convention comes into force, it shall be registered with the Secretary-General of the United Nations by the International Civil Aviation Organization.

ARTICLE 22

1. This Convention shall, after it has come into force, be open for accession by any state Member of the United Nations or of any of the Specialized Agencies.

2. The accession of a state shall be effected by the deposit of an instrument of accession with the International Civil Aviation Organization and shall take effect on the ninetieth day after the date of such deposit.

ARTICLE 23

1. Any Contracting State may denounce this Convention by notification addressed to the International Civil Aviation Organization.

2. Denunciation shall take effect six months after the date of receipt by the International Civil Aviation Organization of the notification of denunciation.

ARTICLE 24

1. Any dispute between two or more Contracting States concerning the interpretation or application of this Convention which cannot be settled through negotiation, shall, at the request of one of them, be submitted to arbitration. If within six months from the date of the request for arbitration the parties are unable to agree on the organization of the arbitration, any one of those parties may refer the dispute to the International Court of Justice by request in conformity with the Statute of the Court.

2. Each state may at the time of signature or ratification of this Convention or accession thereto, declare that it does not consider itself bound by the preceding paragraph. The other Contracting States shall not be bound by the preceding paragraph with respect to any Contracting State having made such a reservation.

3. Any Contracting State having made a reservation in accordance with the preceding paragraph may at any time withdraw this reservation by notification to the International Civil Aviation Organization.

ARTICLE 25

Except as provided in Article 24 no reservation may be made to this Convention.

ARTICLE 26

The International Civil Aviation Organization shall give notice to all states Members of the United Nations or of any of the Specialized Agencies:

(a) of any signature of this Convention and the date thereof;

(b) of the deposit of any instrument of ratification or accession and the date thereof;

(c) of the date on which this Convention comes into force in accordance with Article 21, paragraph 1;

(d) of the receipt of any notification of denunciation and the date thereof; and

(e) of the receipt of any declaration or notification made under Article 24 and the date thereof.

In Witness Whereof the undersigned Plenipotentiaries, having been duly authorized, have signed this Convention.

This Convention shall be deposited with the International Civil Aviation Organization with which, in accordance with Article 19, it shall remain open for signature and the said Organization shall send certified copies thereof to all states Members of the United Nations or of any Specialized Agency.

States Parties

(as of March 1982)

Afghanistan	Chad
Argentina	Chile
Australia	China, Republic of
Austria	Colombia
Bahamas	Congo
Bangladesh	Costa Rica
Barbados	Cyprus
Belgium	Denmark
Bolivia	Dominican Republic
Botswana	Ecuador
Brazil	Egypt
Burundi	El Salvador
Canada	Ethiopia

14

Fiji
Finland
France
Gabon
Gambia
Germany, Federal Republic
   of
Ghana
Greece
Grenada
Guatemala
Guyana
Hungary
Iceland
India
Indonesia
Iran
Iraq
Ireland
Israel
Italy
Ivory Coast
Japan
Jordan
Kenya
Korea, Republic of
Kuwait
Lao Republic
Lebanon
Lesotho
Libya
Luxembourg
Madagascar

Malawi
Mali
Mauritania
Mexico
Morocco
Nepal
Netherlands
New Zealand
Nicaragua
Niger
Nigeria
Norway
Oman
Pakistan
Panama
Papua New Guinea
Paraguay
Peru
Philippines
Poland
Portugal
Romania
Rwanda
Saudi Arabia
Senegal
Seychelles
Sierra Leone
Singapore
South Africa
Spain
Sri Lanka
Surinam
Sweden

Switzerland	United Kingdom
Syria	United States
Thailand	Upper Volta
Togo	Uruguay
Trinidad and Tobago	Vietnam
Tunisia	Yugoslavia
Turkey	Zaire
United Arab Emirates	Zambia

Declarations and Reservations

EGYPT

Egypt does not consider itself bound by paragraph 1 of Article 24.

ETHIOPIA

Ethiopia does not consider itself bound by paragraph 1 of Article 24.

GUATEMALA

Guatemala does not consider itself bound by paragraph 1 of Article 24.

HUNGARY

Hungary does not consider itself bound by paragraph 1 of Article 24.

INDIA

India does not consider itself bound by paragraph 1 of Article 24.

16

INDONESIA

Indonesia does not consider itself bound by paragraph 1 of Article 24.

IRAQ

Accession by the Republic of Iraq shall in no way signify recognition of Israel or entry into any relations with it.

KUWAIT

Accession by Kuwait does not in any way signify recognition of Israel, and no treaty relation will arise between the State of Kuwait and Israel.

MOROCCO

In case of a dispute, all recourse must be made to the International Court of Justice on the basis of the unanimous consent of the parties concerned.

NETHERLANDS

[T]he Convention, with respect to the Kingdom of the Netherlands, shall not enter into force for Surinam and/or the Netherlands Antilles until the ninetieth day after the date on which the Government of the Kingdom of the Netherlands will have notified the International Civil Aviation Organization that in Surinam and/or in the Netherlands Antilles the necessary steps for giving effect to the provisions of the above-mentioned Convention have been taken.

Note: On 4 June 1974 a Declaration dated 10 May 1974 was deposited with the International Civil Aviation Organization by the Government of the Kingdom of the

17

Netherlands stating that the necessary steps for giving effect to the provisions of the Convention had been taken in regard to making the Convention applicable to Surinam and the Netherlands Antilles. Accordingly, the Convention took effect for Surinam and the Netherlands Antilles on 2 September 1974.

OMAN

Oman does not consider itself bound by paragraph 1 of Article 24.

Accession by Oman does not mean or imply, and shall not be interpreted as recognition of Israel generally or in the context of the Convention.

PERU

Peru does not consider itself bound by paragraph 1 of Article 24.

POLAND

Poland does not consider itself bound by paragraph 1 of Article 24.

ROMANIA

Romania does not consider itself bound by paragraph 1 of Article 24.

SOUTH AFRICA

South Africa does not consider itself bound by paragraph 1 of Article 24.

TUNISIA

Tunisia does not consider itself bound by paragraph 1 of Article 24.

UNITED KINGDOM

[T]he provisions of the Convention shall not apply in regard to Southern Rhodesia unless and until the Government of the United Kingdom inform the International Civil Aviation Organization that they are in a position to ensure that the obligations imposed by the Convention in respect of that territory can be fully implemented.

U.S. Action

Message from the President Transmitting the Convention on Offenses and Certain Other Acts Committed on Board Aircraft, S. Exec. Doc. L, 90th Cong., 2nd Sess. (1968).

Convention on Offenses and Certain Other Acts Committed on Board Aircraft: Hearings Before the Senate Commerce Comm., 91st Cong., 2d Sess. (1970).

Senate Comm. on Foreign Relations, Report on the Convention on Offenses and Certain Other Crimes Committed on Board Aircraft, S. Exec. Rep. 9, 91st Cong., 1st Sess. (1969).

Cases

FEDERAL

Court of Appeals

Pan American World Airways, Inc. v. Aetna Casualty & Surety Co., 505 F.2d 989, 1000 (2d Cir. 1974).

United States v. Davis, 482 F.2d 893, 898 (9th Cir. 1973).

United States v. Tiede, 86 F.R.D. 227, 259 (U.S. Ct. for West Berlin (1979).

2. Convention on the Suppression of Unlawful Seizure of Aircraft (Hague Convention), *signed* Dec. 16, 1970, *entered into force* Oct. 14, 1971, 22 U.S.T. 1641, T.I.A.S. No. 7192, 860 U.N.T.S. 105 (*entered into force* for U.S. Oct. 18, 1971).

Editor's Note

The Hague Convention obliges Contracting States to make the offense of unlawful seizure of aircraft punishable by severe penalties (Article 2). The definition provided in Article 1 states that any person commits an offense who on board an aircraft in flight:

> (a) unlawfully, by force or threat thereof, or by any other form of intimidation, seizes, or exercises control of, that aircraft, or attempts to perform any such act; or
> (b) is an accomplice of a person who performs or attempts to perform any such act.

The Convention limits itself to cases where an international element is involved, *i.e.,* where the place of take-off or the place of actual landing of the aircraft on board which the offense is committed is outside the territory of the State of registration of that aircraft. The Convention does not apply to aircraft used in military, customs or police services (Article 3).

Article 4 of the Convention requires the following States to establish jurisdiction: (1) State of registration; (2) State of first landing; and (3) State in which the lessee has its principal place of business or permanent residence. Further, in an attempt to prevent the establishment of safe-havens for hijackers, Article 4 also provides that each Contracting State is to take such measures as may be necessary to establish its jurisdiction over an offense in the case where the alleged offender is present in its territory and is not extradited.

Article 7 embodies the principle *aut dedere aut judicare*, *i.e.*, a Contracting State, if it does not extradite an alleged offender, is obligated to submit his case "without exception whatsoever to its competent authorities for the purpose of prosecution." Although the Convention does not contain an obligation to extradite, it does facilitate the extradition of an alleged offender by providing in Article 8 that the offense referred to in the Convention is deemed to be included as an extraditable offense in any extradition treaty existing between Contracting States and is to be included in every future extradition treaty to be concluded between Contracting States. Further, it is provided that Contracting States may consider the Convention as the legal basis for extradition. Article 8, however, makes it clear that extradition is to be subject to the laws of the requested State, which may preclude extradition of nationals or political offenders.

Text of the Convention

The States Parties to This Convention

Considering that unlawful acts of seizure or exercise of control of aircraft in flight jeopardize the safety of persons and property, seriously affect the operation of air services, and undermine the confidence of the peoples of the world in the safety of civil aviation;

21

Considering that the occurrence of such acts is a matter of grave concern;

Considering that, for the purpose of deterring such acts, there is an urgent need to provide appropriate measures for punishment of offenders;

Have agreed as follows:

ARTICLE 1

Any person who on board an aircraft in flight:

(a) unlawfully, by force or threat thereof, or by any other form of intimidation, seizes, or exercises control of, that aircraft, or attempts to perform any such act, or

(b) is an accomplice of a person who performs or attempts to perform any such act

commits an offence (hereinafter referred to as "the offence").

ARTICLE 2

Each Contracting State undertakes to make the offence punishable by severe penalties.

ARTICLE 3

1. For the purposes of this Convention, an aircraft is considered to be in flight at any time from the moment when all its external doors are closed following embarkation until the moment when any such door is opened for disembarkation. In the case of a forced landing, the flight shall be deemed to continue until the competent authorities take over the responsibility for the aircraft and for persons and property on board.

2. This Convention shall not apply to aircraft used in military, customs or police services.

3. This Convention shall apply only if the place of take-off or the place of actual landing of the aircraft on board which the offence is committed is situated outside the territory of the State of registration of that aircraft; it shall be immaterial whether the aircraft is engaged in an international or domestic flight.

4. In the cases mentioned in Article 5, this Convention shall not apply if the place of take-off and the place of actual landing of the aircraft on board which the offence is committed are situated within the territory of the same State where that State is one of those referred to in that article.

5. Notwithstanding paragraphs 3 and 4 of this article, articles 6, 7, 8 and 10 shall apply whatever the place of take-off or the place of actual landing of the aircraft, if the offender or the alleged offender is found in the territory of a State other than the State of registration of that aircraft.

ARTICLE 4

1. Each Contracting State shall take such measures as may be necessary to establish its jurisdiction over the offence and any other act of violence against passengers or crew committed by the alleged offender in connection with the offence, in the following cases:

(a) when the offence is committed on board an aircraft registered in that State;

(b) when the aircraft on board which the offence is committed lands in its territory with the alleged offender still on board;

(c) when the offence is committed on board an aircraft leased without crew to a lessee who has his principal place of business or, if the lessee has no such place of business, his permanent residence, in that State.

2. Each Contracting State shall likewise take such measures as may be necessary to establish its jurisdiction over the offence in the case where the alleged offender is present in its territory and it does not extradite him pursuant to Article 8 to any of the States mentioned in paragraph 1 of this article.

3. This Convention does not exclude any criminal jurisdiction exercised in accordance with national law.

ARTICLE 5

The Contracting States which establish joint air transport operating organizations or international operating agencies, which operate aircraft which are subject to joint or international registration shall, by appropriate means, designate for each aircraft the State among them which shall exercise the jurisdiction and have the attributes of the State of registration for the purpose of this Convention and shall give notice thereof to the International Civil Aviation Organization which shall communicate the notice to all States Parties to this Convention.

ARTICLE 6

1. Upon being satisfied that the circumstances so warrant, any Contracting State in the territory of which the offender or the alleged offender is present, shall take him into custody or take other measures to ensure his presence. The custody and other measures shall be as provided in the law of that State but may only be continued for such time as is necessary to enable any criminal or extradition proceedings to be instituted.

2. Such State shall immediately make a preliminary inquiry into the facts.

3. Any person in custody pursuant to paragraph 1 of this Article shall be assisted in communicating immediately with the nearest appropriate representative of the State of which he is a national.

4. When a State, pursuant to this Article, has taken a person into custody, it shall immediately notify the State of registration of the aircraft, the State mentioned in Article 4, paragraph 1 (c), the State of nationality of the detained person and, if it considers it advisable, any other interested States of the fact that such person is in custody and of the circumstances which warrant his detention. The State which makes the preliminary inquiry contemplated in paragraph 2 of this Article shall promptly report its findings to the said States and shall indicate whether it intends to exercise jurisdiction.

ARTICLE 7

The Contracting State in the territory of which the alleged offender is found shall, if it does not extradite him, be obliged, without exception whatsoever and whether or not the offence was committed in its territory, to submit the case to its competent authorities for the purpose of prosecution. Those authorities shall take their decision in the same manner as in the case of any ordinary offence of a serious nature under the law of that State.

ARTICLE 8

1. The offence shall be deemed to be included as an extraditable offence in any extradition treaty existing between Contracting States. Contracting States undertake to include the offence as an extraditable offence in every extradition treaty to be concluded between them.

2. If a Contracting State which makes extradition conditional on the existence of a treaty receives a request for extradition from another Contracting State with which it has no extradition treaty, it may at its option consider this Convention as the legal basis for extradition in respect of the offence. Extradition shall be subject to the other conditions provided by the law of the requested State.

3. Contracting States which do not make extradition conditional on the existence of a treaty shall recognize the offence as an extraditable offence between themselves subject to the conditions provided by the law of the requested State.

4. The offence shall be treated, for the purpose of extradition between Contracting States, as if it had been committed not only in the place in which it occurred but also in the territories of the States required to establish their jurisdiction in accordance with Article 4, paragraph 1.

ARTICLE 9

1. When any of the acts mentioned in Article 1 (a) has occurred or is about to occur, Contracting States shall take all appropriate measures to restore control of the aircraft to its lawful commander or to preserve his control of the aircraft.

2. In the cases contemplated by the preceding paragraph, any Contracting State in which the aircraft or its passengers or crew are present shall facilitate the continuation of the journey of the passengers and crew as soon as practicable, and shall without delay return the aircraft and its cargo to the persons lawfully entitled to possession.

Article 10

1. Contracting States shall afford one another the greatest measure of assistance in connection with criminal proceedings brought in respect of the offence and other acts mentioned in Article 4. The law of the State requested shall apply in all cases.

2. The provisions of paragraph 1 of this article shall not affect obligations under any other treaty, bilateral or multilateral, which governs or will govern, in whole or in part, mutual assistance in criminal matters.

Article 11

Each Contracting State shall in accordance with its national law report to the Council of the International Civil Aviation Organization as promptly as possible any relevant information in its possession concerning:

(a) the circumstances of the offence;

(b) the action taken pursuant to Article 9;

(c) the measures taken in relation to the offender or the alleged offender, and, in particular, the results of any extradition proceedings or other legal proceedings.

Article 12

1. Any dispute between two or more Contracting States concerning the interpretation or application of this Convention which cannot be settled through negotiation, shall, at the request of one of them, be submitted to arbitration. If within six months from the date of the request for arbitration the Parties are unable to agree on the organization of the arbitration, any one of those Parties may refer the dispute to the International Court of Justice by request in conformity with the Statute of the Court.

2. Each State may at the time of signature or ratification of this Convention or accession thereto, declare that it does not consider itself bound by the preceding paragraph. The other Contracting States shall not be bound by the preceding paragraph with respect to any Contracting State having made such a reservation.

3. Any Contracting State having made a reservation in accordance with the preceding paragraph may at any time withdraw this reservation by notification to the Depositary Governments.

ARTICLE 13

1. This Convention shall be open for signature at The Hague on 16 December 1970, by States participating in the International Conference on Air Law held at The Hague from 1 to 16 December 1970 (hereinafter referred to as The Hague Conference). After 31 December 1970, the Convention shall be open to all States for signature in Moscow, London and Washington. Any State which does not sign this Convention before its entry into force in accordance with paragraph 3 of this article may accede to it at any time.

2. This Convention shall be subject to ratification by the signatory States. Instruments of ratification and instruments of accession shall be deposited with the Governments of the Union of Soviet Socialist Republics, the United Kingdom of Great Britain and Northern Ireland, and the United States of America, which are hereby designated the Depositary Governments.

3. This Convention shall enter into force thirty days following the date of the deposit of instruments of ratification by ten States signatory to this Convention which participated in The Hague Conference.

4. For other States, this Convention shall enter into force on the date of entry into force of this Convention in accor-

dance with paragraph 3 of this Article, thirty days following the date of deposit of their instruments of ratification or accession, whichever is later.

5. The Depositary Governments shall promptly inform all signatory and acceding States of the date of each signature, the date of deposit of each instrument of ratification or accession, the date of entry into force of this Convention, and other notices.

6. As soon as this Convention comes into force, it shall be registered by the Depositary Governments pursuant to Article 102 of the Charter of the United Nations and pursuant to Article 83 of the Convention on International Civil Aviation (Chicago, 1944).

ARTICLE 14

1. Any Contracting State may denounce this Convention by written notification to the Depositary Governments.

2. Denunciation shall take effect six months following the date on which notification is received by the Depositary Governments.

States Parties

(as of 1 March 1982)

Afghanistan	Benin
Argentina	Bolivia
Australia	Botswana
Austria	Brazil
Bahamas	Bulgaria
Bangladesh	Byelorussian S.S.R.
Barbados	Canada
Belgium	Cape Verde

Chad
Chile
China, People's Republic of
China, Republic of
Colombia
Costa Rica
Cyprus
Czechoslovakia
Denmark
Ecuador
Egypt
El Salvador
Ethiopia
Fiji
Finland
France
Gabon
Gambia
German Democratic Republic
Germany, Federal Republic of
Ghana
Greece
Grenada
Guinea-Bissau
Guyana
Hungary
Iceland
Indonesia
Iran
Iraq
Ireland

Israel
Italy
Ivory Coast
Japan
Jordan
Kenya
Korea, Republic of
Kuwait
Lebanon
Lesotho
Liberia
Libya
Luxembourg
Malawi
Mali
Mauritania
Mexico
Mongolia
Morocco
Nepal
Netherlands
New Zealand
Nicaragua
Niger
Nigeria
Norway
Oman
Pakistan
Panama
Papua New Guinea
Paraguay
Peru
Philippines

Poland	Thailand
Portugal	Togo
Qatar	Tonga
Romania	Trinidad and Tobago
Saudi Arabia	Tunisia
Senegal	Turkey
Seychelles	Uganda
Sierra Leone	Ukrainian S.S.R.
Singapore	U.S.S.R.
South Africa	United Arab Emirates
Spain	United Kingdom
Sri Lanka	United States
Sudan	Uruguay
Surinam	Vietnam
Sweden	Yugoslavia
Switzerland	Zaire
Syria	

Declarations and Reservations

ARGENTINA

The application of this Convention to territories the sovereignty of which may be disputed among two or more States, whether Parties to the Convention or not, may not be interpreted as alteration, renunciation, or waiver of the position upheld by each at the present time.

BRAZIL

Brazil does not consider itself bound by paragraph 1 of Article 12.

BULGARIA

Bulgaria does not consider itself bound by paragraph 1 of Article 12.

BYELORRUSSIAN S.S.R.

Byelorussian S.S.R. does not consider itself bound by paragraph 1 of Article 12.

CHINA, PEOPLE'S REPUBLIC OF

The People's Republic of China does not consider itself bound by paragraph 1, Article 12.

The Chinese Government declares illegal and null and void the signature and ratification of the Hague and Montreal Conventions by the Taiwan authorities in the name of China.

Note: By circular note dated 18 November 1980, the Secretary of State of the United States of America set forth the view of the Government of the United States of America, as a party to the Hague and Montreal Conventions, with respect to the membership of China in these Conventions, as follows:

> In the view of the Government of the United States, China has been and will continue to be a party to the Hague and Montreal Conventions. The Government of the United States recognizes the People's Republic of China as the sole legal Government of China, with whom the Government of the United States will have a treaty relationship under both the Hague and Montreal Conventions.

CZECHOSLOVAKIA

Czechoslovakia does not consider itself bound by paragraph 1 of Article 12.

DENMARK

Until later decision, the Convention will not be applied to the Faroe Islands or to Greenland.

EGYPT

Egypt does not consider itself bound by paragraph 1 of Article 12.

ETHIOPIA

Ethiopia does not consider itself bound by paragraph 1 of Article 12.

GERMANY, FEDERAL REPUBLIC OF

[T]he said Convention shall also apply to Berlin (West) with effect from the date on which it enters into force for the Federal Republic of Germany, on the understanding that:

The rights and responsibilities of the powers responsible for Berlin in the field of civil aviation shall remain unaffected.

The respective competent town commandant shall be entitled in each case to decide in accordance with Article 8 of the Convention whether his nationals may be extradited.

The Allied Kommandatura shall be entitled to determine in accordance with Article 11 of the Convention which authorities will be responsible for reporting to the International Civil Aviation Organization information on seizures of aircraft and any actions taken in connection therewith.

For the purposes of Article 7 of the Convention Law No. 7 of the Allied Kommandatura and the legislation related thereto shall be an integral part of the law in force in Berlin.

HUNGARY

Hungary does not consider itself bound by paragraph 1 of Article 12.

INDONESIA

Indonesia does not consider itself bound by paragraph 1 of Article 12.

IRAQ

Entry into the Convention in no way signifies recognition of Israel or establishes any relations with Israel under the provisions of the Convention.

KOREA, REPUBLIC OF

The accession by the Government of the Republic Korea to the present Convention does not in any way mean or imply the recognition of any territory or regime which has not been recognized by the Government of the Republic of Korea as State or Government.

KUWAIT

Ratification of the Convention does not mean in any way recognition of Israel by the State of Kuwait, and no treaty relations will arise between the State of Kuwait and Israel.

LIBYA

Accession should in no way be regarded as recognition of or establishment of relations with Israel.

MALAWI

Malawi does not consider itself bound by paragraph 1 of Article 12.

MONGOLIA

Mongolia does not consider itself bound by the provisions of Article 12, paragraph 1.

MOROCCO

In case of a dispute, all recourse must be made to the International Court of Justice on the basis of the unanimous consent of the parties concerned.

PAPUA NEW GUINEA

Papua New Guinea does not consider itself bound by paragraph 1 of Article 12.

PERU

Peru does not consider itself bound by paragraph 1 of Article 12.

POLAND

Poland does not consider itself bound by paragraph 1 of Article 12.

QATAR

Upon reviewing and accepting this Convention, we decided with this document to accept, to adhere and promise to observe its rules; however, we state our reservations on the rule of compulsory arbitration stipulated in Article 12 of this convention.

ROMANIA

Romania does not consider itself bound by paragraph 1 of Article 12.

SAUDI ARABIA

Saudi Arabia does not consider itself bound by paragraph 1 of Article 12.

Approval of the Convention by Saudi Arabia does not mean or imply, and shall not be interpeted as, recognition of Israel generally or in the context of this Convention.

SOUTH AFRICA

South Africa does not consider itself bound by paragraph 1 of Article 12.

SYRIA

Syria does not consider itself bound by paragraph 1 of Article 12.

TUNISIA

A dispute may be referred to the International Court of Justice upon agreement of all parties to the dispute.

Ukrainian S.S.R.

Ukrainian S.S.R. does not consider itself bound by paragraph 1 of Article 12.

U.S.S.R.

The U.S.S.R. does not consider itself bound by paragraph 1 of Article 12.

U.S. Action

Message from the President Transmitting the Convention for the Suppression of Unlawful Seizure of Aircraft, S. Exec. Doc. A, 92d Cong., 1st Sess. (1971).

Aircraft Hijacking Convention: Hearings Before the Senate Foreign Relations Comm., 92d Cong., 1st Sess. (1971).

Senate Comm. on Foreign Relations, Report on the Aircraft Hijacking Convention, S. Exec. Rep. 8, 92d Cong., 1st Sess. (1971).

Cases

Federal

Court of Appeals

United States v. Gumerlock, 590 F.2d 794, 796 (9th Cir. 1979).

Pan American World Airways, Inc. v. Aetna Casualty & Surety Co., 505 F.2d 989, 1000 (2d Cir. 1974).

United States v. Davis, 482 F.2d 893, 898 n.10 (9th Cir. 1973).

3. Convention for the Suppression of Unlawful Acts Against the Safety of Civil Aviation (Montreal Convention), *signed* Sept. 23, 1971, *entered into force* Jan. 26, 1973, 24 U.S.T. 564, T.I.A.S. No. 7570 (*entered into force* for U.S. Feb. 28, 1973).

Editor's Note

While the Hague Convention is concerned only with hijacking of aircraft as such, the Montreal Convention covers a broad range of offenses which under Article 3 are to be punishable by "severe penalties." These offenses, outlined in Article 1, include: (1) any acts of violence against a person on board an aircraft in flight; destruction of, or damage to an aircraft in service; sabotage of an aircraft in service; destruction of, or damage to air navigation facilities or interference with their operation; communication of false information which is likely to endanger the safety of aircraft in flight; (2) any attempt to commit any of the aforementioned acts; and (3) any complicity with anyone committing or attempting to commit these acts.

The Convention applies only if:

(a) the place of take-off or landing, actual or intended, of the aircraft is situated outside the territory of the State of registration of that aircraft; or

(b) the offense is committed in the territory of a State other than the State of registration of the aircraft.

(Article 4). Notwithstanding the above provisions, the Convention applies if the alleged offender is found in the territory of a State other than the State of registration of the aircraft (Article 4). The Convention does not apply to aircraft used in military, customs or police services.

The Convention attempts to establish a form of universal jurisdiction. It recognizes, in addition to the traditional territorial jurisdiction, the jurisdiction of: (1) the State of registration; (2) the State of first landing; (3) the State in which the lessee has its principal place of business or permanent residence in the case of an aircraft leased without crew; and (4) the State where the alleged offender is present and is not extradited (Article 5).

Like the Hague Convention, the Montreal Convention contains the principle of *aut dedere aut judicare, i.e.,* the Contracting States have an obligation either to extradite the alleged offender found in their territory or to submit his case, without exception whatsoever, to their competent authorities for the purpose of prosecution (Article 7).

While Convention contains provisions (similar to the Hague Convention) for the facilitation of extradition, it does not create an obligation to extradite (Article 8).

Text of the Convention

The States Parties to this Convention

Considering that unlawful acts against the safety of civil aviation jeopardize the safety of persons and property, seriously affect the operation of air services, and undermine the confidence of the peoples of the world in the safety of civil aviation;

Considering that the occurrence of such acts is a matter of grave concern;

Considering that, for the purpose of deterring such acts, there is an urgent need to provide appropriate measures for punishment of offenders;

Have Agreed as Follows:

ARTICLE 1

1. Any person commits an offence if he unlawfully and intentionally:

(a) performs an act of violence against a person on board an aircraft in flight if that act is likely to endanger the safety of that aircraft; or

(b) destroys an aircraft in service or causes damage to such an aircraft which renders it incapable of flight or which is likely to endanger its safety in flight; or

(c) places or causes to be placed on an aircraft in service, by any means whatsoever, a device or substance which is likely to destroy that aircraft, or to cause damage to it which renders it incapable of flight, or to cause damage to it which is likely to endanger its safety in flight; or

(d) destroys or damages air navigation facilities or interferes with their operation, if any such act is likely to endanger the safety of aircraft in flight; or

(e) communicates information which he knows to be false, thereby endangering the safety of an aircraft in flight.

2. Any person also commits an offence if he:

(a) attempts to commit any of the offences mentioned in paragraph 1 of this Article; or

(b) is an accomplice of a person who commits or attempts to commit any such offence.

ARTICLE 2

For the purposes of this Convention:

(a) an aircraft is considered to be in flight at any time from the moment when all its external doors are closed following embarkation until the moment when any such door is opened for disembarkation; in the case of a forced landing the flight shall be deemed to continue until the competent authorities take over the responsibility for the aircraft and for persons and property on board;

(b) an aircraft is considered to be in service from the beginning of the preflight preparation of the aircraft by ground personnel or by the crew for a specific flight until twenty-four hours after any landing; the period of service shall, in any event, extend for the entire period during which the aircraft is in flight as defined in paragraph (a) of this Article.

ARTICLE 3

Each Contracting State undertakes to make the offences mentioned in Article 1 punishable by severe penalties.

ARTICLE 4

1. This Convention shall not apply to aircraft used in military, customs or police services.

2. In the cases contemplated in subparagraphs (a), (b), (c) and (e) of paragraph 1 of Article 1, this Convention shall apply, irrespective of whether the aircraft is engaged in an international or domestic flight, only if:

(a) the place of take-off or landing, actual or intended, of the aircraft is situated outside the territory of the State of registration of that aircraft; or

(b) the offence is committed in the territory of a State other than the State of registration of the aircraft.

3. Notwithstanding paragraph 2 of this Article, in the cases contemplated in subparagraphs (a), (b), (c) and (e) of paragraph 1 of Article 1, this Convention shall also apply if the offender or the alleged offender is found in the territory of a State other than the State of registration of the aircraft.

4. With respect to the States mentioned in Article 9 and in the cases mentioned in subparagraphs (a), (b), (c) and (e)

of paragraph 1 of Article 1, this Convention shall not apply if the places referred to in subparagraph (a) of paragraph 2 of this Article are situated within the territory of the same State where that State is one of those referred to in Article 9, unless the offence is committed or the offender or alleged offender is found in the territory of a State other than that State.

5. In the cases contemplated in subparagraph (d) of paragraph 1 of Article 1, this Convention shall apply only if the air navigation facilities are used in international air navigation.

6. The provisions of paragraphs 2, 3, 4 and 5 of this Article shall also apply in the cases contemplated in paragraph 2 of Article 1.

ARTICLE 5

1. Each Contracting State shall take such measures as may be necessary to establish its jurisdiction over the offences in the following cases:

(a) when the offence is committed in the territory of that State;

(b) when the offence is committed against or on board an aircraft registered in that State;

(c) when the aircraft on board which the offence is committed lands in its territory with the alleged offender still on board;

(d) when the offence is committed against or on board an aircraft leased without crew to a lessee who has his principal place of business or, if the lessee has no such place of business, his permanent residence, in that State.

2. Each Contracting State shall likewise take such measures as may be necessary to establish its jurisdiction over the offences mentioned in Article 1, paragraph 1 (a), (b) and

(c), and in Article 1, paragraph 2, in so far as that paragraph relates to those offences, in the case where the alleged offender is present in its territory and it does not extradite him pursuant to Article 8 to any of the States mentioned in paragraph 1 of this Article.

3. This Convention does not exclude any criminal jurisdiction exercised in accordance with national law.

ARTICLE 6

1. Upon being satisfied that the circumstances so warrant, any Contracting State in the territory of which the offender or the alleged offender is present, shall take him into custody or take other measures to ensure his presence. The custody and other measures shall be as provided in the law of that State but may only be continued for such time as is necessary to enable any criminal or extradition proceedings to be instituted.

2. Such State shall immediately make a preliminary inquiry into the facts.

3. Any person in custody pursuant to paragraph 1 of this Article shall be assisted in communicating immediately with the nearest appropriate representative of the State of which he is a national.

4. When a State, pursuant to this Article, has taken a person into custody, it shall immediately notify the States mentioned in Article 5, paragraph 1, the State of nationality of the detained person and, if it considers it advisable, any other interested States of the fact that such person is in custody and of the circumstances which warrant his detention. The State which makes the preliminary inquiry contemplated in paragraph 2 of this Article shall promptly report its findings to the said States and shall indicate whether it intends to exercise jurisdiction.

ARTICLE 7

The Contracting State in the territory of which the alleged offender is found shall, if it does not extradite him, be obliged, without exception whatsoever and whether or not the offence was committed in its territory, to submit the case to its competent authorities for the purpose of prosecution. Those authorities shall take their decision in the same manner as in the case of any ordinary offence of a serious nature under the law of that State.

ARTICLE 8

1. The offences shall be deemed to be included as extraditable offences in any extradition treaty existing between Contracting States. Contracting States undertake to include the offences as extraditable offences in every extradition treaty to be concluded between them.

2. If a Contracting State which makes extradition conditional on the existence of a treaty receives a request for extradition from another Contracting State with which it has no extradition treaty, it may at its option consider this Convention as the legal basis for extradition in respect of the offences. Extradition shall be subject to the conditions provided by the law of the requested State.

3. Contracting States which do not make extradition conditional on the existence of a treaty shall recognize the offences as extraditable offences between themselves subject to the conditions provided by the law of the requested State.

4. Each of the offences shall be treated, for the purpose of extradition between Contracting States, as if it had been committed not only in the place in which it occurred but also in the territories of the States required to establish their jurisdiction in accordance with Article 5, paragraph 1 (b), (c) and (d).

ARTICLE 9

The Contracting States which establish joint air transport operating organizations or international operating agencies, which operate aircraft which are subject to joint or international registration shall, by appropriate means, designate for each aircraft the State among them which shall exercise the jurisdiction and have the attributes of the State of registration for the purpose of this Convention and shall give notice thereof to the International Civil Aviation Organization which shall communicate the notice to all States Parties to this Convention.

ARTICLE 10

1. Contracting States shall, in accordance with international and national law, endeavour to take all practicable measures for the purpose of preventing the offences mentioned in Article 1.

2. When, due to the commission of one of the offences mentioned in Article 1, a flight has been delayed or interrupted, any Contracting State in whose territory the aircraft or passengers or crew are present shall facilitate the continuation of the journey of the passengers and crew as soon as practicable, and shall without delay return the aircraft and its cargo to the persons lawfully entitled to possession.

ARTICLE 11

1. Contracting States shall afford one another the greatest measure of assistance in connection with criminal proceedings brought in respect of the offences. The law of the State requested shall apply in all cases.

45

2. The provisions of paragraph 1 of this Article shall not affect obligations under any other treaty, bilateral or multilateral, which governs or will govern, in whole or in part, mutual assistance in criminal matters.

ARTICLE 12

Any Contracting State having reason to believe that one of the offences mentioned in Article 1 will be committed shall, in accordance with its national law, furnish any relevant information in its possession to those States which it believes would be the States mentioned in Article 5, paragraph 1.

ARTICLE 13

Each Contracting State shall in accordance with its national law report to the Council of the International Civil Aviation Organization as promptly as possible any relevant information in its possession concerning:

(a) the circumstances of the offence;

(b) the action taken pursuant to Article 10, paragraph 2;

(c) the measures taken in relation to the offender or the alleged offender and, in particular, the results of any extradition proceedings or other legal proceedings.

ARTICLE 14

1. Any dispute between two or more Contracting States concerning the interpretation or application of this Convention which cannot be settled through negotiation, shall, at the request of one of them, be submitted to arbitration. If within six months from the date of the request for arbitration the Parties are unable to agree on the organization

of the arbitration, any one of those Parties may refer the dispute to the International Court of Justice by request in conformity with the Statute of the Court.

2. Each State may at the time of signature or ratification of this Convention or accession thereto, declare that it does not consider itself bound by the preceding paragraph. The other Contracting States shall not be bound by the preceding paragraph with respect to any Contracting State having made such a reservation.

3. Any Contracting State having made a reservation in accordance with the preceding paragraph may at any time withdraw this reservation by notification to the Depositary Governments.

ARTICLE 15

1. This Convention shall be open for signature at Montreal on 23 September 1971 by States participating in the International Conference on Air Law held at Montreal from 8 to 23 September 1971 (hereinafter referred to as the Montreal Conference). After 10 October 1971, the Convention shall be open to all States for signature in Moscow, London and Washington. Any State which does not sign this Convention before its entry into force in accordance with paragraph 3 of this Article may accede to it at any time.

2. This Convention shall be subject to ratification by the signatory States. Instruments of ratification and instruments of accession shall be deposited with the Governments of the Union of Soviet Socialist Republics, the United Kingdom of Great Britain and Northern Ireland, and the United States of America, which are hereby designated the Depositary Governments.

3. This Convention shall enter into force thirty days following the date of the deposit of instruments of ratification by ten States signatory to this Convention which participated in the Montreal Conference.

4. For other States, this Convention shall enter into force on the date of entry into force of this Convention in accordance with paragraph 3 of this Article, or thirty days following the date of deposit of their instruments of ratification or accession, whichever is later.

5. The Depositary Governments shall promptly inform all signatory and acceding States of the date of each signature, the date of deposit of each instrument of ratification or accession, the date of entry into force of this Convention, and other notices.

6. As soon as this Convention comes into force, it shall be registered by the Depositary Governments pursuant to Article 102 of the Charter of the United Nations, and pursuant to Article 83 of the Convention on International Civil Aviation (Chicago, 1944).

ARTICLE 16

1. Any Contracting State may denounce this Convention by written notification to the Depositary Governments.

2. Denunciation shall take effect six months following the date on which notification is received by the Depositary Governments.

States Parties

(as of 1 March 1982)

Argentina	Bolivia
Australia	Brazil
Austria	Bulgaria
Bangladesh	Byelorussian S.S.R.
Barbados	Cameroon
Belgium	Canada

Cape Verde
Chad
Chile
China, Republic of
China, People's Republic of
Colombia
Costa Rica
Cyprus
Czechoslovakia
Denmark
Dominican Republic
Ecuador
Egypt
El Salvador
Ethiopia
Fiji
Finland
France
Gabon
Gambia
German Democratic
  Republic
Germany, Federal Republic
  of
Ghana
Grenada
Greece
Guatemala
Guinea-Bissau
Guyana
Hungary
Iceland
Indonesia

Iran
Iraq
Ireland
Israel
Italy
Ivory Coast
Japan
Jordan
Kenya
Korea, Republic of
Korea, People's Democratic
  Republic of
Kuwait
Lebanon
Lesotho
Liberia
Libya
Malawi
Mali
Mauritania
Mexico
Mongolia
Morocco
Nepal
Netherlands
New Zealand
Nicaragua
Niger
Nigeria
Norway
Oman
Pakistan
Panama

Papua New Guinea
Paraguay
Peru
Philippines
Poland
Portugal
Qatar
Romania
Saudi Arabia
Senegal
Seychelles
Sierra Leone
Singapore
South Africa
Spain
Sri Lanka
Sudan
Surinam

Sweden
Switzerland
Syria
Thailand
Togo
Tonga
Trinidad and Tobago
Turkey
Tunisia
Ukrainian S.S.R.
U.S.S.R.
United Arab Emirates
United Kingdom
United States
Uruguay
Vietnam
Yugoslavia
Zaire

Declarations and Reservations

BRAZIL

Brazil does not consider itself bound by paragraph 1 of Article 14.

BULGARIA

Bulgaria does not consider itself bound by paragraph 1 of Article 14.

BYELORUSSIAN S.S.R.

Byelorussian S.S.R. does not consider itself bound by paragraph 1 of Article 14.

CAMEROON

Accession by Cameroon was accompanied by a note of 10 July 1973, which stated that in view of the fact that Cameroon did not have any relations with South Africa and Portugal, it did not have any obligation towards these two countries with regard to the implementation of the Convention.

Note: By note of 6 December 1977, Cameroon declared that, having established diplomatic relations with Portugal on 12 February 1977, it withdrew the declaration made against Portugal. Cameroon also stated that the position with regards to South Africa remained.

CHINA, PEOPLE'S REPUBLIC OF

The People's Republic of China does not consider itself bound by paragraph 1, Article 14.

The Chinese Government declares illegal and null and void the signature and ratification of the Hague and Montreal Conventions by the Taiwan authorities in the name of China.

Note: By circular note dated 18 November 1980, the Secretary of State of the United States of America set forth the view of the Government of the United States of America, as a party to the Hague and Montreal Conventions, with respect to the membership of China in these Conventions, as follows:

In the view of the Government of the United States, China has been and will continue to be a party to the Hague and Montreal Conventions. The Government of the United States recognizes the People's Republic of China as the sole legal Goverment of China, with whom the Government of the United States will have a treaty relationship under both the Hague and Montreal Conventions.

Czechoslovakia

Czechoslovakia does not consider itself bound by paragraph 1 of Article 14.

Denmark

Until a later decision, the Convention will not be applied to the Faroe Islands and to Greenland.

Egypt

Egypt does not consider itself bound by paragraph 1 of Article 14.

Ethiopia

Ethiopia does not consider itself bound by paragraph 1 of Article 14.

France

France does not consider itself bound by paragraph 1 of Article 14.

German Democratic Republic

The German Democratic Republic does not consider itself bound by paragraph 1 of Article 14.

Germany, Federal Republic of

[T]he said Convention shall also apply to Berlin (West) with effect from the date on which it enters into force for the Federal Republic of Germany, on the understanding that:

The rights and responsibilities of the Powers responsible for Berlin in the field of civil aviation shall remain unaffected.

The respective competent sector Commandant shall be entitled in each case to decide in accordance with Article 8 of the Convention whether his nationals may be extradited.

The Allied Kommandatura shall be entitled to determine in accordance with Article 13 of the Convention which authorities will be responsible for reporting to the International Civil Aviation Organization on the circumstances of the unlawful acts and any actions taken in connexion therewith.

For the purposes of Article 7 of the Convention Law No. 7 of the Allied Kommandatura and the legislation related thereto is an integral part of the law in force in Berlin.

GUATEMALA

Guatemala does not consider itself bound by paragraph 1 of Article 14.

HUNGARY

Hungary does not consider itself bound by paragraph 1 of Article 14.

INDONESIA

Indonesia does not consider itself bound by paragraph 1 of Article 14.

KOREA, REPUBLIC OF

Accession by the Republic of Korea does not in any way mean or imply the recognition of any territory or regime which has not been recognized by the Government of Korea as a State or Government.

KUWAIT

Accession by Kuwait does not in any way signify recognition, and no treaty relation will arise between the State of Kuwait and Israel.

MALAWI

Malawi does not consider itself bound by paragraph 1 of Article 14.

MONGOLIA

Mongolia does not consider itself bound by paragraph 1 of Article 14.

MOROCCO

In case of a dispute, all recourse must be made to the International Court of Justice on the basis of the unanimous consent of the parties concerned.

OMAN

Oman does not consider itself bound by paragraph 1 of Article 14.

Accession by Oman does not mean or imply, and shall not be interpreted as recognition of Israel generally or in the context of this convention.

Papua New Guinea

Papua New Guinea does not consider itself bound by paragraph 1 of Article 14.

Peru

Peru does not consider itself bound by paragraph 1 of Article 14.

Poland

Poland does not consider itself bound by paragraph 1 of Article 14.

Qatar

Upon reviewing and accepting this Convention, we decided with this document to accept, adhere and promise to observe its rules; however, we state our reservation on the rule of compulsory arbitration stipulated in Article 14 of this Convention.

Romania

Romania does not consider itself bound by paragraph 1 of Article 14.

Romania considers null and void the signing of the Convention by the so called Chiang-Kai-Shek authorities in so far as the only government having the right to assume obligations on behalf of China and to represent her in international relations is the Government of the People's Republic of China.

SAUDI ARABIA

Saudi Arabia does not consider itself bound by paragraph 1 of Article 14.

Accession by Saudia Arabia does not mean or imply, and shall not be interpreted as, recognition of Israel generally or in the context of this Convention.

SOUTH AFRICA

South Africa does not consider itself bound by paragraph 1 of Article 14.

SYRIA

Syria does not consider itself bound by paragraph 1 of Article 14.

TUNISIA

A dispute may be referred to the International Court of Justice upon agreement of all parties to the dispute.

UKRAINIAN S.S.R.

Ukrainian S.S.R. does not consider itself bound by paragraph 1 of Article 14.

U.S.S.R.

The U.S.S.R. does not consider itself bound by paragraph 1 of Article 14.

United Kingdom

The Convention is ratified in respect of the United Kingdom of Great Britain and Northern Ireland and Territories under the territorial sovereignty of the United Kingdom, as well as the British Solomon Islands Protecterate.

Vietnam

Vietnam does not consider itself bound by paragraph 1 of Article 14.

U.S. Action

Message from the President Transmitting the Convention for the Suppression of Unlawful Acts Against the Safety of Civil Aviation, S. Exec. Doc. T, 92d Cong., 2d Sess. (1972).

Senate Comm. on Foreign Relations, Report on the Aircraft Sabotage Convention, S. Exec. Rep. 34, 92d Cong., 2d Sess. (1972).

Cases

Federal

Court of Appeals

United States v. Davis, 482 F.2d 893, 898 n.10 (9th Cir. 1973).

4. Convention on the Prevention and Punishment of Crimes against Internationally Protected Persons, Including Diplomatic Agents (New York Convention), *adopted* Dec. 14, 1973, *entered into force* Feb. 20, 1977,

28 U.S.T. 1975, T.I.A.S. No. 8532, G.A. Res. 3166, 28 U.N. GAOR Supp. (No. 30) 146, U.N. Doc. A/9030 (1974) (*entered into force* for U.S. Mar. 18, 1977).

Editor's Note

The New York Convention in Article 2 obliges Contracting States to make punishable by appropriate penalties the following acts against "internationally protected persons" (as defined under Article 1):

(a) murder, kidnapping, or other attack upon the person or liberty of an internationally protected person;

(b) a violent attack upon the official premises, the private accommodation or the means of transport of an internationally protected person likely to endanger his person or liberty;

(c) a threat to commit any such attack;

(d) an attempt to commit any such attack; and

(e) an act constituting participation as an accomplice in any such act.

Article 3 provides that each Contracting State is to "take such measures as may be necessary to establish its jurisdiction over the crimes" referred to in the Convention when:

(a) the crime is committed in the territory of that State or on board a ship or aircraft registered in that State;

(b) the alleged offender is a national of that State; [and]

(c) the crime is committed against an internationally protected person who enjoys his status as such by virtue of functions which he exercises on behalf of that State.

Article 7, like the Hague and Montreal Conventions, embodies the principle of *aut dedere aut judicare, i.e.,* a State is obliged either to extradite an accused offender or submit his case to its competent authorities for prosecution.

For extradition purposes, the crimes referred to in the Convention are deemed to be included as extraditable offenses under any extradition treaty existing between Contracting States and are to be included in every future extradition treaty to be concluded between Contracting States (Article 8). As for States that do not make extradition conditional on the existence of a treaty, they are obliged to recognize these crimes as extraditable offenses between themselves subject to the procedural provisions and the other conditions of the law of the requested State. Further, it is provided that Contracting States may consider the Convention as the legal basis for extradition (Article 6).

States Parties are obliged under Article 10 to "afford one another the greatest measure of assistance in connexion with criminal proceedings brought in respect of the crimes set forth in [the Convention], including the supply of all evidence at their disposal necessary for the proceedings."

The provisions of the Convention do not affect the application of the treaties on asylum in force at the date of its adoption (Article 12).

Text of the Convention

[Editor's Note: The General Assembly's resolution adopting the New York Convention is reprinted below. Although the Resolution's text "decides" that any reprint of the Convention include the accompanying Resolution, Iraq is the only State to regard the Resolution as an integral part of the Convention.]

The General Assembly,

Considering that the codification and progressive development of international law contributes to the implementation of the purposes and principles set forth in Articles 1 and 2 of the Charter of the United Nations,

Recalling, that in response to the request made in General Assembly resolution 2780 (XXVI) of 3 December 1971, the International Law Commission, at its twenty-fourth session, studied the question of the protection and inviolability of diplomatic agents and other persons entitled to special protection under international law and prepared draft articles on the prevention and punishment of crimes against such persons,

Having considered the draft articles and also the comments and observations thereon submitted by States, specialized agencies and other intergovernmental organizations in response to the invitation extended by the General Assembly in its resolution 2926 (XXVII) of 28 November 1972,

Convinced of the importance of securing international agreement on appropriate and effective measures for the prevention and punishment of crimes against diplomatic agents and other internationally protected persons in view of the serious threat to the maintenance and promotion of friendly relations and co-operation among States created by the commission of such crimes,

Having elaborated for that purpose the provisions contained in the Convention annexed thereto,

1. *Adopts* the Convention on the Prevention and Punishment of Crimes against Internationally Protected Persons, including Diplomatic Agents, annexed to the present resolution;

2. *Re-emphasizes* the great importance of the rules of international law concerning the inviolability of and special protection to be afforded to internationally protected persons and the obligations of States in relation thereto;

3. *Considers* that the annexed Convention will enable States to carry out their obligations more effectively;

4. *Recognizes* also that the provisions of the annexed Convention could not in any way prejudice the exercise of the legitimate right to self-determination and independence, in accordance with the purposes and principles of the Charter of the United Nations and the Declaration of Principles of International Law concerning Friendly Relations and Co-operation among States in accordance with the Charter of the United Nations, by people struggling against colonialism, alien domination, foreign occupation, racial discrimination and *apartheid;*

5. *Invites* States to become parties to the annexed Convention;

6. *Decides* that the present resolution, whose provisions are related to the annexed Convention, shall always be published together with it.

The States Parties to this Convention,

Having in mind the purposes and principles of the Charter of the United Nations concerning the maintenance of international peace and the promotion of friendly relations and co-operation among States,

Considering that crimes against diplomatic agents and other internationally protected persons jeopardizing the safety of these persons create a serious threat to the maintenance of normal international relations which are necessary for co-operation among States,

Believing that the commission of such crimes is a matter of grave concern to the international community,

Convinced that there is an urgent need to adopt appropriate and effective measures for the prevention and punishment of such crimes,

Have agreed as follows:

ARTICLE 1

For the purposes of this Convention:

1. "Internationally protected person" means:

(a) A Head of State, including any member of a collegial body performing the functions of a Head of State under the constitution of the State concerned, a Head of Government or a Minister for Foreign Affairs, whenever any such person is in a foreign State, as well as members of his family who accompany him;

(b) Any representative or official of a State or any official or any agent of an international organization of an intergovernmental character who, at the time when and in the place where a crime against him, his official premises, his private accommodation or his means of transport is committed, is entitled pursuant to international law to special protection from any attack on his person, freedom or dignity, as well as members of his family forming part of his household;

2. "Alleged offender" means a person as to whom there is sufficient evidence to determine *prima facie* that he has committed or participated in one or more of the crimes set forth in Article 2.

ARTICLE 2

1. The intentional commission of:

(a) A murder, kidnapping or other attack upon the person or liberty of an internationally protected person;

(b) A violent attack upon the official premises, the private accommodation or the means of transport of an internationally protected person likely to endanger his person or liberty;

(c) A threat to commit any such attack;

(d) An attempt to commit any such attack; and

(e) An act constituting participation as an accomplice in any such attack shall be made by each State Party a crime under its internal law.

2. Each State Party shall make these crimes punishable by appropriate penalties which take into account their grave nature.

3. Paragraphs 1 and 2 of this article in no way derogate from the obligations of States Parties under international law to take all appropriate measures to prevent other attacks on the person, freedom or dignity of an internationally protected person.

ARTICLE 3

1. Each State Party shall take such measures as may be necessary to establish its jurisdiction over the crimes set forth in article 2 in the following cases:

(a) When the crime is committed in the territory of that State or on board a ship or aircraft registered in that State;

(b) When the alleged offender is a national of that State;

(c) When the crime is committed against an internationally protected person as defined in article 1 who enjoys his status as such by virtue of functions which he exercises on behalf of that State.

2. Each State Party shall likewise take such measures as may be necessary to establish its jurisdiction over these crimes in cases where the alleged offender is present in its territory and it does not extradite him pursuant to article 8 to any of the States mentioned in paragraph 1 of this article.

3. This Convention does not exclude any criminal jurisdiction exercised in accordance with internal law.

ARTICLE 4

States Parties shall co-operate in the prevention of the crimes set forth in article 2, particularly by:

(a) Taking all practicable measures to prevent preparations in their respective territories for the commission of those crimes within or outside their territories;

(b) Exchanging information and co-ordinating the taking of administrative and other measures as appropriate to prevent the commission of those crimes.

ARTICLE 5

1. The State Party in which any of the crimes set forth in article 2 has been committed shall, if it has reason to believe that an alleged offender has fled from its territory, communicate to all other States concerned, directly or through the Secretary-General of the United Nations, all the pertinent facts regarding the crime committed and all available information regarding the identity of the alleged offender.

2. Whenever any of the crimes set forth in article 2 has been committed against an internationally protected person, any State Party which has information concerning the victim and the circumstances of the crime shall endeavour to transmit it, under the conditions provided for in its internal law, fully and promptly to the State Party on whose behalf he was exercising his functions.

ARTICLE 6

1. Upon being satisfied that the circumstances so warrant, the State Party in whose territory the alleged offender is present shall take the appropriate measures under its internal law so as to ensure his presence for the

purpose of prosecution or extradition. Such measures shall be notified without delay directly or through the Secretary-General of the United Nations to:

(a) The State where the crime was committed;

(b) The State or States of which the alleged offender is a national or, if he is a stateless person, in whose territory he permanently resides;

(c) The State or States of which the internationally protected person concerned is a national or on whose behalf he was exercising his functions;

(d) All other States concerned; and

(e) The international organization of which the internationally protected person concerned is an official or an agent.

2. Any person regarding whom the measures referred to in paragraph 1 of this article are being taken shall be entitled:

(a) to communicate without delay with the nearest appropriate representative of the State of which he is a national or which is otherwise entitled to protect his rights or, if he is a stateless person, which he requests and which is willing to protect his rights; and

(b) to be visited by a representative of that State.

ARTICLE 7

The State Party in whose territory the alleged offender is present shall, if it does not extradite him, submit, without exception whatsoever and without undue delay, the case to its competent authorities for the purpose of prosecution, through proceedings in accordance with the laws of that State.

ARTICLE 8

1. To the extent that the crimes set forth in article 2 are not listed as extraditable offenses in any extradition treaty existing between States Parties, they shall be deemed to be included as such therein. States Parties undertake to include those crimes as extraditable offences in every future extradition treaty to be concluded between them.

2. If a State Party which makes extradition conditional on the existence of a treaty receives a request for extradition from another State Party with which it has no extradition treaty, it may, if it decides to extradite, consider this Convention as the legal basis for extradition in respect of those crimes. Extradition shall be subject to the procedural provisions and the other conditions of the law of the requested State.

3. States Parties which do not make extradition conditional on the existence of a treaty shall recognize those crimes as extraditable offences between themselves subject to the procedural provisions and the other conditions of the law of the requested State.

4. Each of the crimes shall be treated, for the purpose of extradition between States Parties, as if it had been committed not only in the place in which it occurred but also in the territories of the States required to establish their jurisdiction in accordance with paragraph 1 of article 3.

ARTICLE 9

Any person regarding whom proceedings are being carried out in connection with any of the crimes set forth in article 2 shall be guaranteed fair treatment at all stages of the proceedings.

ARTICLE 10

1. States Parties shall afford one another the greatest measure of assistance in connection with criminal proceedings brought in respect of the crimes set forth in article 2, including the supply of all evidence at their disposal necessary for the proceedings.

2. The provisions of paragraph 1 of this article shall not affect obligations concerning mutual judicial assistance embodied in any other treaty.

ARTICLE 11

The State Party where an alleged offender is prosecuted shall communicate the final outcome of the proceedings to the Secretary-General of the United Nations, who shall transmit the information to the other States Parties.

ARTICLE 12

The provisions of this Convention shall not affect the application of the Treaties on Asylum, in force at the date of the adoption of this Convention, as between the States which are parties to those Treaties, but a State Party to this Convention may not invoke those Treaties with respect to another State Party to this Convention which is not a party to those Treaties.

ARTICLE 13

1. Any dispute between two or more States Parties concerning the interpretation or application of this Convention which is not settled by negotiation shall, at the request of one of them, be submitted to arbitration. If within six months from the date of the request for arbitration the parties are unable to agree on the organization of the arbi-

tration, any one of those parties may refer the dispute to the International Court of Justice by request in conformity with the Statute of the Court.

2. Each State Party may at the time of signature or ratification of this Convention or accession thereto declare that it does not consider itself bound by paragraph 1 of this article. The other States Parties shall not be bound by paragraph 1 of this article with respect to any State Party which has made such a reservation.

3. Any State Party which has made a reservation in accordance with paragraph 2 of this article may at any time withdraw that reservation by notification to the Secretary-General of the United Nations.

ARTICLE 14

This Convention shall be open for signature by all States, until 31 December 1974 at United Nations Headquarters in New York.

ARTICLE 15

This Convention is subject to ratification. The instruments of ratification shall be deposited with the Secretary-General of the United Nations.

ARTICLE 16

This Convention shall remain open for accession by any State. The instruments of accession shall be deposited with the Secretary-General of the United Nations.

ARTICLE 17

1. This Convention shall enter into force on the thirtieth day following the date of deposit of the twenty-second instrument of ratification or accession with the Secretary-General of the United Nations.

2. For each State ratifying or acceding to the Convention after the deposit of the twenty-second instrument of ratification or accession, the Convention shall enter into force on the thirtieth day after deposit by such State of its instrument of ratification or accession.

ARTICLE 18

1. Any State Party may denounce this Convention by written notification to the Secretary-General of the United Nations.

2. Denunciation shall take effect six months following the date on which notification is received by the Secretary-General of the United Nations.

ARTICLE 19

The Secretary-General of the United Nations shall inform all States, *inter alia:*

(a) Of signatures to this Convention, of the deposit of instruments of ratification or accession in accordance with articles 14, 15 and 16 and of notifications made under article 18;

(b) Of the date on which this Convention will enter into force in accordance with article 17.

ARTICLE 20

The original of this Convention, of which the Chinese, English, French, Russian and Spanish texts are equally authentic, shall be deposited with the Secretary-General of the United Nations, who shall send certified copies thereof to all States.

States Parties

(as of 1 March 1982)

Australia	Haiti
Austria	Hungary
Barbados	Iceland
Bulgaria	India
Burundi	Israel
Byelorussian S.S.R.	Iran
Canada	Iraq
Chile	Jamaica
Costa Rica	Liberia
Cyprus	Malawi
Czechoslovakia	Mexico
Denmark	Mongolia
Dominican Republic	Nicaragua
Ecuador	Norway
El Salvador	Pakistan
Finland	Panama
Gabon	Paraguay
German Democratic	Peru
Republic	Philippines
Germany, Federal Republic	Romania
of	Rwanda
Ghana	Seychelles

Sweden	United Kingdom
Togo	U.S.S.R.
Trinidad and Tobago	United States
Tunisia	Uruguay
Turkey	Yugoslavia
Ukrainian S.S.R.	Zaire

Declarations and Reservations

BULGARIA

Bulgaria does not consider itself bound by the provisions of article 13, paragraph 1, of the Convention, under which any dispute between two or more States Parties concerning the interpretation or application of the Convention shall, at the request of one of them, be submitted to arbitration or to the International Court of Justice, and states that, in each individual case, the consent of all parties to such a dispute is necessary for submission of the dispute to arbitration or to the International Court of Justice.

BYELORUSSIAN S.S.R.

The Byelorussian Soviet Socialist Republic does not consider itself bound by the provisions of article 13, paragraph 1, of the Convention, under which any dispute between two or more States Parties concerning the interpretation or application of the Convention shall, at the request of one of them, be submitted to arbitration or to the International Court of Justice, and states that, in each individual case, the consent of all parties to such a dispute is necessary for submission of the dispute to arbitration or to the International Court of Justice.

CZECHOSLOVAKIA

Czechoslovakia does not feel itself bound by the provisions of article 13, paragraph 1, of the Convention.

ECUADOR

Ecuador wishes to avail itself of the provisions of article 13, paragraph 2, of the Convention, declaring that it does not consider itself bound to refer disputes concerning the application of the Convention to the International Court of Justice.

EL SALVADOR

The State of El Salvador does not consider itself bound by paragraph 1 of article 13 of the Convention.

FINLAND

Finland reserves the right to apply the provision of article 8, paragraph 3, in such a way that extradition shall be restricted to offences which, under Finnish Law, are punishable by a penalty more severe than imprisonment for one year and, provided also that other conditions in the Finnish Legislation for extradition are fulfilled.

Finland also reserves the right to make such other reservations as it may deem appropriate if and when ratifying this Convention.

GERMAN DEMOCRATIC REPUBLIC

The German Democratic Republic does not regard itself bound by the provisions of article 13, paragraph 1, and reaffirms its view that in conformity with the principle of the sovereign equality of States the approval of all parties to any dispute is required in order to subject a certain dispute to arbitration or to submit it to decision to the International Court of Justice.

GERMANY, FEDERAL REPUBLIC OF

The Federal Republic of Germany reserves the right, upon ratifying this Convention, to state its views on the explanations of votes and declarations made by other States upon signing or ratifying or acceding to that Convention and to make reservations regarding certain provisions of the said Convention.

GHANA

Paragraph 1 of article 13 of the Convention provides that disputes may be submitted to arbitration, failing which any of the parties to the dispute may refer it to the International Court of Justice by request. Since Ghana is opposed to any form of compulsory arbitration, she wishes to exercise her option under article 13(2) to make a reservation on article 13(1). It is noted that such a reservation can be withdrawn later under article 13(3).

Note: By notification received on 18 November 1976, the Government of Ghana informed the Secretary-General that it has decided to withdraw the reservation as contained in its instrument of accession, concerning article 3(1)(c) of the said Convention. That reservation reads as follows:

(i) Paragraph 1(c) of article 3 of the Convention contemplates that a State may exercise jurisdiction when the crime is committed against its own agent. This may lead to some friction with the State in whose territory the crime has been committed or the State whose national the offender is. It may also not afford the offender a fair trial. Ghana therefore wishes to make a reservation on article 3(1)(c) of the Convention.

73

HUNGARY

The Hungarian People's Republic does not consider itself bound by the provisions of article 13, paragraph 1, of the Convention. These provisions are at variance with the position of the Hungarian People's Republic according to which for the submission of disputes between States to arbitration or to the International Court of Justice the consent of all of the interested parties is required.

INDIA

The Government of the Republic of India does not consider itself bound by paragraph 1 of article 13 which establishes compulsory arbitration or adjudication by the International Court of Justice concerning disputes between two or more States Parties relating to the interpretation or application of this Convention.

IRAQ

(1) The resolution of the United Nations General Assembly with which the above-mentioned Convention is enclosed shall be considered to be an integral part of the above-mentioned Convention.

(2) Sub-paragraph (B) of paragraph (1) of article 1 of the Convention shall cover the representatives of the national liberation movements recognized by the League of Arab States or the Organization of African Unity.

(3) The Republic of Iraq shall not bind itself by paragraph (1) of article 13 of the Convention.

(4) The accession of the Government of the Republic of Iraq to the Convention shall in no way constitute a recognition of Israel or a cause for the establishment of any relations of any kind therewith.

ISRAEL

The State of Israel does not consider itself bound by paragraph 1 of article 13 of the Convention.

The Government of the State of Israel does not regard as valid the reservation made by Iraq in respect of paragraph (1) (b) of article 1 of the said Convention.

The Government of the State of Israel declares that its accession to the Convention does not constitute acceptance by it as binding of the provisions of any other international instrument, or acceptance by it of any other international instrument as being an instrument related to the Convention.

The Government of Israel reaffirms the contents of its communication of 11 May 1979 to the Secretary-General of the United Nations.

JAMAICA

Jamaica avails itself of the provisions of article 13, paragraph 2, and declares that it does not consider itself bound by the provisions of paragraph 1 of this article under which any dispute between two or more States Parties concerning the interpretation of application of this Convention shall, at the request of one of them, be submitted to arbitration or referred to the International Court of Justice, and states that in each individual case, the consent of all parties to such a dispute is necessary for the submission of the dispute to arbitration or to the International Court of Justice.

MALAWI

The Government of the Republic of Malawi [declares], in accordance with the provisions of paragraph 2 of Article 13, that it does not consider itself bound by the provisions of paragraph 1 of article 13 of the Convention.

MONGOLIA

The Mongolian People's Republic does not consider itself bound by the provisions of article 13, paragraph 1, of the Convention, under which any dispute between two or more States Parties concerning the interpretation or application of the Convention shall, at the request of one of them, be submitted to arbitration or to the International Court of Justice, and states that, in each individual case, the consent of all parties to such a dispute is necessary for submission of the dispute to arbitration or to the International Court of Justice.

PAKISTAN

Pakistan shall not be bound by paragraph 1 of article 13 of the Convention.

PERU

With reservation as to article 13(1).

ROMANIA

The Socialist Republic of Romania declares that it does not consider itself bound by the provisions of article 13, paragraph 1, of the Convention, under which any dispute between two or more Contracting Parties concerning the interpretation or application of the Convention which is not settled by negotiation shall, at the request of one of them, be submitted to arbitration or referred to the International Court of Justice.

The Socialist Republic of Romania considers that such disputes may be submitted to arbitration or referred to the International Court of Justice only with the consent of all parties to the dispute in each individual case.

TRINIDAD AND TOBAGO

The Republic of Trinidad and Tobago avails itself of the provision of Article 13, paragraph 2, and declares that it does not consider itself bound by the provisions of paragraph 1 of that Article under which any dispute between two or more States Parties concerning the interpretation or application of this Convention shall, at the request of one of them, be submitted to arbitration or referred to the International Court of Justice, and states that in each individual case, the consent of all parties to such a dispute is necessary for the submission of the dispute to arbitration or to the International Court of Justice.

TUNISIA

No dispute may be brought before the International Court of Justice unless by agreement between all parties to the dispute.

UKRAINIAN S.S.R.

The Ukrainian Soviet Socialist Republic does not consider itself bound by the provisions of article 13, paragraph 1, of the Convention, under which any dispute between two or more States Parties concerning the interpretation or application of the Convention shall, at the request of one of them, be submitted to arbitration or to the International Court of Justice, and states that, in each individual case, the consent of all parties to such a dispute is necessary for submission of the dispute to arbitration or to the International Court of Justice.

U.S.S.R.

The Union of Soviet Socialist Republics does not consider itself bound by the provisions of article 13, paragraph 1, of the Convention, under which any dispute between two or more States Parties concerning the interpretation or application of the Convention shall, at the request of one of them, be submitted to arbitration or to the International Court of Justice, and states that, in each individual case, the consent of all parties to such a dispute is necessary for submission of the dispute to arbitration or to the International Court of Justice.

ZAIRE

The Republic of Zaire does not consider itself bound by the provisions of article 13, paragraph 1, of the Convention, under which any dispute between two or more Contracting Parties concerning the interpretation or application of the Convention which is not settled by negotiation shall, at the request of one of them, be submitted to arbitration or referred to the International Court of Justice. In the light of its policy based on respect for the sovereignty of States, the Republic of Zaire is opposed to any form of compulsory arbitration and hopes that such disputes may be submitted to arbitration or referred to the International Court of Justice not at the request of one of the parties but with the consent of all the interested parties.

U.S. Action

Message from the President Transmitting the Convention on the Prevention and Punishment of Crimes Against Internationally Protected Persons, S. Exec. Doc. L, 93d Cong., 2d Sess. (1974).

Senate Comm. on Foreign Relations, Report on the Convention on the Prevention and Punishment of Crimes Against Internationally Protected Persons, S. Exec. Rep. 10, 94th Cong., 1st Sess. (1975).

Cases

FEDERAL

District Court

United States v. Layton, 509 F. Supp. 212, 222-25 (N.D. Cal. 1981).

5. Convention to Prevent and Punish the Acts of Terrorism Taking the Forms of Crime Against Persons and Related Extortion That Are of International Significance, *signed* Feb. 2, 1971, *entered into force* Oct. 16, 1973, 27 U.S.T. 3949, T.I.A.S. No. 8413 (*entered into force* for U.S. Oct. 20, 1976).

Editor's Note

Although establishing in Article 1 a duty for Contracting States to cooperate in the prevention and punishment of "acts of terrorism," this O.A.S. Convention does not actually deal with terrorism as a whole. Its focus is on terrorist acts, characterized in Article 2 as common crimes of international significance, namely, kidnapping, murder and other assaults against the life or personal integrity of those persons to whom the State has the duty to give special protection according to international law, as well as extortion in connection with those crimes.

Article 8 of the Convention obliges States to include in their penal laws the above prohibited acts. While Article 6 safeguards the right to asylum, Article 5 embodies the principle of *aut dedere aut judicare, i.e.,* a State is obliged either to extradite an accused offender or submit his case to its competent authorities for prosecution. Extradition is to be granted pursuant to extradition treaties in force between the Contracting States or, in the case of States that do not make extradition dependent upon the existence of a treaty, in accordance with the conditions established by the laws of the requested State (Articles 3 & 7).

The Convention also is open to participation by States which are not members of the Organization of American States.

Text of the Convention

Whereas:

The defence of freedom and justice and respect for the fundamental rights of the individual that are recognized by the American Declaration of the Rights and Duties of Man and the Universal Declaration of Human Rights are primary duties of States;

The General Assembly of the Organization, in resolution 4, of 30 June 1970, strongly condemned acts of terrorism, especially the kidnapping of persons and extortion in connection with that crime, which it declared to be serious common crimes;

Criminal acts against persons entitled to special protection under international law are occurring frequently, and those acts are of international significance because of the consequences that may flow from them for relations among States;

It is advisable to adopt general standards that will progressively develop international law as regards co-operation in the prevention and punishment of such acts; and

In the application of those standards the institution of asylum should be maintained and, likewise the principle of non-intervention should not be impaired,

THE MEMBER STATES OF THE ORGANIZATION OF AMERICAN STATES HAVE AGREED UPON THE FOLLOWING ARTICLES:

ARTICLE 1

The Contracting States undertake to co-operate among themselves by taking all the measures that they may consider effective, under their own laws, and especially those established in this convention, to prevent and punish acts of terrorism, especially kidnapping, murder, and other assaults against the life or physical integrity of those persons to whom the State has the duty according to international law to give special protection, as well as extortion in connection with those crimes.

ARTICLE 2

For the purposes of this Convention, kidnapping, murder and other assaults against the life or personal integrity of those persons to whom the State has the duty to give special protection according to international law, as well as extortion in connection with those crimes, shall be considered common crimes of international significance, regardless of motive.

ARTICLE 3

Persons who have been charged or convicted for any of the crimes referred to in Article 2 of this Convention shall be subject to extradition under the provisions of the extradition treaties in force between the parties or, in the

81

case of States that do not make extradition dependent on the existence of a treaty, in accordance with their own laws.

In any case, it is the exclusive responsibility of the State under whose jurisdiction or protection such persons are located to determine the nature of the acts and decide whether the standards of this Convention are applicable.

ARTICLE 4

Any person deprived of his freedom through the application of this Convention shall enjoy the legal guarantees of due process.

ARTICLE 5

When extradition requested for one of the crimes specified in Article 2 is not in order because the person sought is a national of the requested State, or because of some other legal or constitutional impediment, that State is obliged to submit the case to its competent authorities for prosecution, as if the act had been committed in its territory. The decision of these authorities shall be communicated to the State that requested extradition. In such proceedings, the obligation established in Article 4 shall be respected.

ARTICLE 6

None of the provisions of this Convention shall be interpreted so as to impair the right of asylum.

ARTICLE 7

The Contracting States undertake to include the crimes referred to in Article 2 of this Convention among the punishable acts giving rise to extradition in any treaty on the subject to which they agree among themselves in the future. The Contracting States that do not subject extradition to the existence of a treaty with the requesting State shall consider the crimes referred to in Article 2 of this Convention as crimes giving rise to extradition, according to the conditions established by the laws of the requested State.

ARTICLE 8

To co-operate in preventing and punishing the crimes contemplated in Article 2 of this Convention, the Contracting States accept the following obligations:

(a) To take all measures within their power, and in conformity with their own laws, to prevent and impede the preparation in their respective territories of the crimes mentioned in Article 2 that are to be carried out in the territory of another Contracting State.

(b) To exchange information and consider effective administrative measures for the purpose of protecting the persons to whom Article 2 of this Convention refers.

(c) To guarantee to every person deprived of his freedom through the application of this Convention every right to defend himself.

(d) To endeavour to have the criminal acts contemplated in this Convention included in their penal laws, if not already so included.

(e) To comply most expeditiously with the requests for extradition concerning the criminal acts contemplated in this Convention.

ARTICLE 9

This Convention shall remain open for signature by the member States of the Organization of American States, as well as by any other State that is a Member of the United

Nations or any of its specialized agencies, or any State that is a party to the Statute of the International Court of Justice, or any other State that may be invited by the General Assembly of the Organization of American States to sign it.

ARTICLE 10

This Convention shall be ratified by the signatory States in accordance with their respective constitutional procedures.

ARTICLE 11

The original instrument of this Convention, the English, French, Portuguese, and Spanish texts of which are equally authentic, shall be deposited in the General Secretariat of the Organization of American States, which shall send certified copies to the signatory Governments for purposes of ratification. The instruments of ratification shall be deposited in the General Secretariat of the Organization of American States, which shall notify the signatory Governments of such deposit.

ARTICLE 12

This Convention shall enter into force among the states that ratify it when they deposit their respective instruments of ratification.

ARTICLE 13

This Convention shall remain in force indefinitely, but any of the Contracting States may denounce it. The denunciation shall be transmitted to the General

Secretariat of the Organization of American States, which shall notify the other Contracting States thereof. One year following the denunciation, the Convention shall cease to be in force for the denouncing State, but shall continue to be in force for the other Contracting States.

States Parties

(as of 1 March 1982)

Costa Rica
Dominican Republic
Mexico
Nicaragua
United States
Uruguay
Venezuela

U.S. Action

Message from the President Transmitting the Convention to Prevent and Punish the Acts of Terrorism Taking the Forms of Crime Against Persons and Related Extortion That Are of International Significance, S. Exec. Doc. D, 92d Cong., 1st Sess. (1971).

Senate Comm. on Foreign Relations, Report on the Convention to Prevent and Punish the Acts of Terrorism Taking the Forms of Crime Against Persons and Related Extortion That Are of International Significance, S. Exec. Rep. 23, 92d Cong., 2d Sess. (1972).

Cases

FEDERAL

District Court

Tel-Oren v. Libyan Arab Republic, 517 F. Supp. 542, 546 (D.D.C. 1981).

United States v. Layton, 509 F. Supp. 212, 222 (N.D. Cal. 1981).

6. International Convention Against the Taking of Hostages, *adopted* Dec. 17, 1979, G.A. Res. 34/146, 34 U.N. GAOR Supp. (No. 39), U.N. Doc. A/34/819 (1979), *reprinted in* 18 Int'l Legal Materials 1457 (1979).

Editor's Note

The Convention stipulates that each State Party shall make the attempted or actual taking of hostages punishable by appropriate penalties "which take into account the grave nature of the offense" (Article 2). Article 3 obligates the State Party in the territory of which hostages are held to take all measures it considers appropriate to ease the situation of the hostages, and to return any objects coming into its hands which an offender has obtained as a result of the taking of hostages. Article 5 compels each State Party to take such actions as may be necessary to establish jurisdiction over specific situations involving the taking of hostages.

Under Article 8, a State Party is obligated to initiate measures to take an alleged offender found in its territory into custody and then either directly or through the UN Secretary-General notify all other States concerned. The individual in custody is entitled to communicate with the nearest appropriate representative of his State and to be visited by a representative of that State (Article 8).

The State Party in the territory of which the alleged offender is found is obligated either to extradite or prosecute him (Article 8). A request for extradition is not to be granted if the requested state has substantial grounds for believing that the request has been made for the purpose of prosecuting or punishing a person on account of his race, religion, nationality, ethnic origin or political opinion. The request is also to be denied if the state believes that the individual may be prejudiced against for those reasons (Article 9). The provisions on extradition supersede all extradition treaties and arrangements to the extent that they are incompatible with the Convention (Article 9).

Article 12 provides that the Convention is inapplicable to acts of hostage-taking to which the Geneva Convention of 1949 or its Additional Protocols apply. The Convention also does not affect the application of the treaties on asylum in force on the date of the adoption of the Convention between States which are parties to those treaties. However, a State Party may not invoke those treaties with respect to another State Party not a party to those treaties (Article 15).

Under Article 16, any dispute between two or more States Parties will be submitted to arbitration at the request of one of them.

Text of the Convention

The States Parties to this Convention,

Having in mind the purposes and principles of the Charter of the United Nations concerning the maintenance of international peace and security and the promotion of friendly relations and co-operation among States,

Recognizing in particular that everyone has the right to life, liberty and security of person, as set out in the Universal Declaration of Human Rights and the International Covenant on Civil and Political Rights,

Reaffirming the principle of equal rights and self- determination of peoples as enshrined in the Charter of the

United Nations and the Declaration on Principles of International Law concerning Friendly Relations and Co-operation among States in accordance with the Charter of the United Nations, as well as in other relevant resolutions of the General Assembly,

Considering that the taking of hostages is an offence of grave concern to the international community and that, in accordance with the provisions of this Convention, any person committing an act of hostage taking shall be either prosecuted or extradited,

Being convinced that it is urgently necessary to develop international co-operation between States in devising and adopting effective measures for the prevention, prosecution and punishment of all acts of taking hostages as manifestations of international terrorism,

Have agreed as follows:

ARTICLE 1

1. Any person who seizes or detains and threatens to kill, to injure or to continue to detain another person (hereinafter referred to as the "hostage") in order to compel a third party, namely, a State, an international intergovernmental organization, a natural or juridical person, or a group of persons, to do or abstain from doing any act as an explicit or implicit condition for the release of the hostage commits the offence of taking of hostages ("hostage-taking") within the meaning of this Convention.

2. Any person who:

(a) attempts to commit an act of hostage-taking, or

(b) participates as an accomplice of anyone who commits or attempts to commit an act of hostage-taking likewise commits an offense for the purposes of this Convention.

ARTICLE 2

Each State Party shall make the offences set forth in article 1 punishable by appropriate penalties which take into account the grave nature of those offences.

ARTICLE 3

1. The State Party in the territory of which the hostage is held by the offender shall take all measures it considers appropriate to ease the situation of the hostage, in particular, to secure his release and, after his release, to facilitate, when relevant, his departure.

2. If any object which the offender has obtained as a result of the taking of hostages comes into the custody of a State Party, that State Party shall return it as soon as possible to the hostage or the third party referred to in article 1, as the case may be, or to the appropriate authorities thereof.

ARTICLE 4

States Parties shall co-operate in the prevention of the offences set forth in article 1, particularly by:

(a) taking all practicable measures to prevent preparations in their respective territories for the commission of those offences within or outside their territories, including measures to prohibit in their territories illegal activities of persons, groups and organizations that encourage, instigate, organize or engage in the perpetration of acts of taking of hostages;

89

(b) exchanging information and co-ordinating the taking of administrative and other measures as appropriate to prevent the commission of those offences.

ARTICLE 5

1. Each State Party shall take such measures as may be necessary to establish its jurisdiction over any of the offences set forth in article 1 which are committed:

(a) in its territory or on board a ship or aircraft registered in that State;

(b) by any of its nationals or, if that State considers it appropriate, by those stateless persons who have their habitual residence in its territory;

(c) in order to compel that State to do or abstain from doing any act; or

(d) with respect to a hostage who is a national of that State, if that State considers it appropriate.

2. Each State Party shall likewise take such measures as may be necessary to establish its jurisdiction over the offences set forth in article 1 in cases where the alleged offender is present in its territory and it does not extradite him to any of the States mentioned in paragraph 1 of this article.

3. This Convention does not exclude any criminal jurisdiction exercised in accordance with internal law.

ARTICLE 6

1. Upon being satisfied that the circumstances so warrant, any State Party in the territory of which the alleged offender is present shall, in accordance with its laws, take him into custody or take other measures to ensure his presence for such time as is necessary to enable

any criminal or extradition proceedings to be instituted. That State Party shall immediately make a preliminary inquiry into the facts.

2. The custody or other measures referred to in paragraph 1 of this article shall be notified without delay directly or through the Secretary-General of the United Nations to:

(a) the State where the offence was committed;

(b) the State against which compulsion has been directed or attempted;

(c) the State of which the natural or juridical person against whom compulsion has been directed or attempted is a national;

(d) the State of which the hostage is a national or in the territory of which he has his habitual residence;

(e) the State of which the alleged offender is a national or, if he is a stateless person, in the territory of which he has his habitual residence;

(f) the international intergovernmental organization against which compulsion has been directed or attempted;

(g) all other States concerned.

3. Any person regarding whom the measures referred to in paragraph 1 of this article are being taken shall be entitled:

(a) to communicate without delay with the nearest appropriate representative of the State of which he is a national or which is otherwise entitled to establish such communication or, if he is a stateless person, the State in the territory of which he has his habitual residence;

(b) to be visited by a representative of that State.

4. The rights referred to in paragraph 3 of this article shall be exercised in conformity with the laws and regulations of the State in the territory of which the alleged offender is present, subject to the proviso, however, that the said laws and regulations must enable full effect to be given to the purposes for which the rights accorded under paragraph 3 of this article are intended.

5. The provisions of paragraphs 3 and 4 of this article shall be without prejudice to the right of any State Party having a claim to jurisdiction in accordance with paragraph 1 (b) of article 5 to invite the International Committee of the Red Cross to communicate with and visit the alleged offender.

6. The State which makes the preliminary inquiry contemplated in paragraph 1 of this article shall promptly report its findings to the States or organization referred to in paragraph 2 of this article and indicate whether it intends to exercise jurisdiction.

ARTICLE 7

The State Party where the alleged offender is prosecuted shall in accordance with its laws communicate the final outcome of the proceedings to the Secretary-General of the United Nations, who shall transmit the information to the other States concerned and the international intergovernmental organizations concerned.

ARTICLE 8

1. The State Party in the territory of which the alleged offender is found shall, if it does not extradite him, be obliged, without exception whatsoever and whether or not the offence was committed in its territory, to submit the case to its competent authorities for the purpose of prosecu-

tion, through proceedings in accordance with the laws of that State. Those authorities shall take their decision in the same manner as in the case of any ordinary offence of a grave nature under the law of that State.

2. Any person regarding whom proceedings are being carried out in connexion with any of the offences set forth in article 1 shall be guaranteed fair treatment at all stages of the proceedings, including enjoyment of all the rights and guarantees provided by the law of the State in the territory of which he is present.

ARTICLE 9

1. A request for the extradition of an alleged offender, pursuant to this Convention, shall not be granted if the requested State Party has substantial grounds for believing:

(a) that the request for extradition for an offence set forth in article 1 has been made for the purpose of prosecuting or punishing a person on account of his race, religion, nationality, ethnic origin or political opinion; or

(b) that the person's position may be prejudiced:

(i) for any of the reasons mentioned in subparagraph (a) of this paragraph, or

(ii) for the reason that communication with him by the appropriate authorities of the State entitled to exercise rights of protection cannot be effected.

2. With respect to the offences as defined in this Convention, the provisions of all extradition treaties and arrangements applicable between States Parties are modified as between States Parties to the extent that they are incompatible with this Convention.

ARTICLE 10

1. The offences set forth in article 1 shall be deemed to be included as extraditable offences in any extradition treaty existing between States Parties. States Parties undertake to include such offences as extraditable offences in every extradition treaty to be concluded between them.

2. If a State Party which makes extradition conditional on the existence of a treaty receives a request for extradition from another State Party with which it has no extradition treaty, the requested State may at its option consider this Convention as the legal basis for extradition in respect of the offences set forth in article 1. Extradition shall be subject to the other conditions provided by the law of the requested State.

3. States Parties which do not make extradition conditional on the existence of a treaty shall recognize the offences set forth in article 1 as extraditable offences between themselves subject to the conditions provided by the law of the requested State.

4. The offences set forth in article 1 shall be treated, for the purpose of extradition between States Parties, as if they had been committed not only in the place in which they occurred but also in the territories of the States required to establish their jurisdiction in accordance with paragraph 1 of article 5.

ARTICLE 11

1. States Parties shall afford one another the greatest measure of assistance in connexion with criminal proceedings brought in respect of the offences set forth in article 1, including the supply of all evidence at their disposal necessary for the proceedings.

2. The provisions of paragraph 1 of this article shall not affect obligations concerning mutual judicial assistance embodied in any other treaty.

ARTICLE 12

In so far as the Geneva Conventions of 1949 for the protection of war victims or the Additional Protocols to those Conventions are applicable to a particular act of hostage-taking, and in so far as States Parties to this Convention are bound under those conventions to prosecute or hand over the hostage-taker, the present Convention shall not apply to an act of hostage-taking committed in the course of armed conflicts as defined in the Geneva Conventions of 1949 and the Protocols thereto, including armed conflicts mentioned in article 1, paragraph 4, of Additional Protocol I of 1977, in which peoples are fighting against colonial domination and alien occupation and against racist régimes in the exercise of their right of self-determination, as enshrined in the Charter of the United Nations and the Declaration on Principles of International Law concerning Friendly Relations and Co-operation among States in accordance with the Charter of the United Nations.

ARTICLE 13

This Convention shall not apply where the offence is committed within a single State, the hostage and the alleged offender are nationals of that State and the alleged offender is found in the territory of that State.

ARTICLE 14

Nothing in this Convention shall be construed as justifying the violation of the territorial integrity or political independence of a State in contravention of the Charter of the United Nations.

ARTICLE 15

The provisions of this Convention shall not affect the application of the Treaties on Asylum, in force at the date of the adoption of this Convention, as between the States which are parties to those Treaties; but a State Party to this Convention may not invoke those Treaties with respect to another State Party to this Convention which is not a party to those treaties.

ARTICLE 16

1. Any dispute between two or more States Parties concerning the interpretation or application of this Convention which is not settled by negotiation shall, at the request of one of them, be submitted to arbitration. If within six months from the date of the request for arbitration the parties are unable to agree on the organization of the arbitration, any one of those parties may refer the dispute to the International Court of Justice by request in conformity with the Statute of the Court.

2. Each State may at the time of signature or ratification of this Convention or accession thereto declare that it does not consider itself bound by paragraph 1 of this article. The other States Parties shall not be bound by paragraph 1 of this article with respect to any State Party which has made such a reservation.

3. Any State Party which has made a reservation in accordance with paragraph 2 of this article may at any time withdraw that reservation by notification to the Secretary-General of the United Nations.

ARTICLE 17

1. This Convention is open for signature by all States until 31 December 1980 at United Nations Headquarters in New York.

2. This Convention is subject to ratification. The instruments of ratification shall be deposited with the Secretary-General of the United Nations.

3. This Convention is open for accession by any State. The instruments of accession shall be deposited with the Secretary-General of the United Nations.

ARTICLE 18

1. This Convention shall enter into force on the thirtieth day following the date of deposit of the twenty-second instrument of ratification or accession with the Secretary-General of the United Nations.

2. For each State ratifying or acceding to the Convention after the deposit of the twenty-second instrument of ratification or accession, the Convention shall enter into force on the thirtieth day after deposit by such State of its instrument of ratification or accession.

ARTICLE 19

1. Any State Party may denounce this Convention by written notification to the Secretary-General of the United Nations.

2. Denunciation shall take effect one year following the date on which notification is received by the Secretary-General of the United Nations.

ARTICLE 20

The original of this Convention, of which the Arabic, Chinese, English, French, Russian and Spanish texts are equally authentic, shall be deposited with the Secretary-General of the United Nations, who shall send certified copies thereof to all States.

IN WITNESS WHEREOF, the undersigned, being duly authorized thereto by their respective Governments, have signed this Convention, opened for signature at New York on 18 December 1979.

States Parties

(as of 1 March 1982)

Bahamas
Barbados
Bhutan
Chile
El Salvador
Germany, Federal Republic of
Honduras
Iceland
Kenya
Lesotho
Mauritius
Norway
Surinam
Sweden
Trinidad and Tobago

Declarations and Reservations

KENYA

The government of Kenya does not consider itself bound by the provisions of paragraph (1) of the [sic] article 16 of the Convention.

U.S. Action

Message from the President on the International Convention Against the Taking of Hostages, S. Exec. Doc. N, 96th Cong., 2d Sess. (1980).

Senate Comm. on Foreign Relations, Report on the International Convention Against the Taking of Hostages, S. Exec. Rep. 17, 97th Cong., 1st Sess. (1981).

The International Convention Against the Taking of Hostages: Hearings Before the Senate Comm. on Foreign Relations, 97th Cong., 1st Sess. (1981).

7. Geneva Convention Relative to the Protection of Civilian Persons in Time of War of August 12, 1949, *opened for signature* Aug. 12, 1949, *entered into force* Oct. 21, 1950, 6 U.S.T. 3516, T.I.A.S. No. 3365, 75 U.N.T.S. 287 *(entered into force* for U.S. Feb. 2, 1956).

Editor's Note

The Convention contains a peremptory prohibition of all measures of terrorism by Contracting Parties in international conflicts. Article 33 states, *inter alia:* "Collective penalties and likewise all measures of intimidation or of terrorism are prohibited." This provision is technically applicable only to "protected persons" as defined by Article 4:

> Persons protected by the Convention are those who, at a given moment and in any manner whatsoever, find themselves, in case of a conflict or occupation, in the hands of a party to the conflict or Occupying Power of which they are not nationals.

Other humane treatment provisions prohibit specific terrorist acts: violence to life and person (Article 27), cruel treatment (Article 32), torture (Article 32), physical and moral coercion (Article 31), outrages upon personal dignity (Article 27), and the taking of hostages (Article 34).

Most terrorist acts in conflicts not of international character seem to be prohibited by Article 3, which proscribes:

> (a) violence to life and person, in particular murder of all kinds, mutilation, cruel treatment and torture;
> (b) taking of hostages;
> (c) outrages upon personal dignity, in particular humiliating and degrading treatment; [and]
> (d) the passing of sentences and the carrying out of executions without previous judgment pronounced by a regularly constituted court, affording all the judicial guarantees which are recognized as indispensable by civilized peoples.

The Convention requires the Contracting Parties "to undertake to enact any legislation necessary to provide effective penal sanctions for persons committing or ordering to be committed any of the grave breaches . . ." (Article 146). In addition, each Contracting Party is obliged "to search for persons alleged to have committed, or to have ordered to be committed, such grave breaches and shall bring such persons, regardless of their nationality before its own courts" (Article 146). In the alternative, a High Contracting

Party, if it prefers, may hand over such persons for trial to another High Contracting Party, provided the latter has made out a *prima facie* case (Article 146). Jurisdiction to prosecute an alleged offender is therefore universal, but Contracting States are left free either to prosecute or extradite the accused, in accordance with their extradition laws and treaties.

Most acts of terrorism would seem to be included in the concept "grave breaches," for which universal jurisdiction is prescribed. "Grave breaches" refers to acts committed against persons or property protected by the Convention involving, *inter alia:* willful killing; torture or inhumane treatment; willful infliction of great suffering or serious injury to body or health; taking of hostages; and extensive destruction and appropriation of property, not justified by military necessity and carried out unlawfully and wantonly (Article 147).

Text of Selected Articles of the Convention

ARTICLE 3

In the case of armed conflict not of an international character occurring in the territory of one of the High Contracting Parties, each Party to the conflict shall be bound to apply, as a minimum, the following provisions:

(1) Persons taking no active part in the hostilities, including members of armed forces who have laid down their arms and those placed *hors de combat* by sickness, wounds, detention, or any other cause, shall in all circumstances be treated humanely, without any adverse distinction founded on race, colour, religion or faith, sex, birth or wealth, or any other similar criteria.

101

To this end, the following acts are and shall remain prohibited at any time and in any place whatsoever with respect to the above-mentioned persons:

(a) violence to life and person, in particular murder of all kinds, mutilation, cruel treatment and torture;

(b) taking of hostages;

(c) outrages upon personal dignity, in particular humiliating and degrading treatment;

(d) the passing of sentences and the carrying out of executions without previous judgment pronounced by a regularly constituted court, affording all the judicial guarantees which are recognized as indispensable by civilized peoples.

(2) The wounded and sick shall be collected and cared for.

An impartial humanitarian body, such as the International Committee of the Red Cross, may offer its services to the Parties to the conflict.

The Parties to the conflict should further endeavour to bring into force, by means of special agreements, all or part of the other provisions of the present Convention.

The application of the preceding provisions shall not affect the legal status of the Parties to the conflict.

ARTICLE 4

Persons protected by the Convention are those who, at a given moment and in any manner whatsoever, find themselves, in case of a conflict or occupation, in the hands of a Party to the conflict or Occupying Power of which they are not nationals.

Nationals of a State which is not bound by the Convention are not protected by it. Nationals of a neutral State who find themselves in the territory of a belligerent State, and nationals of a co-belligerent State, shall not be regarded as protected persons while the State of which they are nationals has normal diplomatic representation in the State in whose hands they are.

The provisions of Part II are, however, wider in application, as defined in Article 13.

Persons protected by the Geneva Convention for the Amelioration of the Condition of the Wounded and Sick in Armed Forces in the Field of August 12, 1949, or by the Geneva Convention for the Amelioration of the Condition of Wounded, Sick and Shipwrecked Members of Armed Forces at Sea of August 12, 1949, or by the Geneva Convention relative to the Treatment of Prisoners of War of August 12, 1949, shall not be considered as protected persons within the meaning of the present Convention.

ARTICLE 27

Protected persons are entitled, in all circumstances, to respect for their persons, their honour, their family rights, their religious convictions and practices, and their manners and customs. They shall at all times be humanely treated, and shall be protected especially against all acts of violence or threats thereof and against insults and public curiosity.

Women shall be especially protected against any attack on their honour, in particular against rape, enforced prostitution, or any form of indecent assault.

Without prejudice to the provisions relating to their state of health, age and sex, all protected persons shall be treated with the same consideration by the Party to the conflict in whose power they are, without any adverse distinction based, in particular, on race, religion or political opinion.

However, the Parties to the conflict may take such measures of control and security in regard to protected persons as may be necessary as a result of the war.

103

ARTICLE 31

No physical or moral coercion shall be exercised against protected persons, in particular to obtain information from them or from third parties.

ARTICLE 32

The High Contracting Parties specifically agree that each of them is prohibited from taking any measure of such a character as to cause the physical suffering or extermination of protected persons in their hands. This prohibition applies not only to murder, torture, corporal punishment, mutilation and medical or scientific experiments not necessitated by the medical treatment of a protected person, but also to any other measures of brutality whether applied by civilian or military agents.

ARTICLE 33

No protected person may be punished for an offence he or she has not personally committed. Collective penalties and likewise all measures of intimidation or of terrorism are prohibited.

Pillage is prohibited.

Reprisals against protected persons and their property are prohibited.

ARTICLE 34

The taking of hostages is prohibited.

ARTICLE 146

The High Contracting Parties undertake to enact any legislation necessary to provide effective penal sanctions for persons committing, or ordering to be committed, any of the grave breaches of the present Convention defined in the following Article.

Each High Contracting Party shall be under the obligation to search for persons alleged to have committed, or to have ordered to be committed, such grave breaches, and shall bring such persons, regardless of their nationality, before its own courts. It may also, if its prefers, and in accordance with the provisions of its own legislation, hand such persons over for trial to another High Contracting Party concerned, provided such High Contracting Party has made out a *prima facie* case.

Each High Contracting Party shall take measures necessary for the suppression of all acts contrary to the provisions of the present Convention other than the grave breaches defined in the following Article.

In all circumstances, the accused persons shall benefit by safeguards of proper trial and defence, which shall not be less favourable than those provided by Article 105 and those following of the Geneva Convention relative to the Treatment of Prisoners of War of August 12, 1949.

ARTICLE 147

Grave breaches to which the preceding Article relates shall be those involving any of the following acts, if committed against persons or property protected by the present Convention: wilful killing, torture or inhuman treatment, including biological experiments, wilfully causing great suffering or serious injury to body or health, unlawful deportation or transfer or unlawful confinement of

105

a protected person, compelling a protected person to serve in the forces of a hostile Power, or wilfully depriving a protected person of the rights of fair and regular trial prescribed in the present Convention, taking of hostages and extensive destruction and appropriation of property, not justified by military necessity and carried out unlawfully and wantonly.

States Parties

(as of 1 March 1982)

Afghanistan
Albania
Algeria
Argentina
Australia
Austria
Bahamas
Bahrain
Bangladesh
Barbados
Belgium
Benin
Bolivia
Botswana
Brazil
Bulgaria
Burundi
Byelorussian S.S.R.
Cameroon
Canada
Central African Republic

Chad
Chile
China, People's Republic of
Colombia
Congo
Costa Rica
Cuba
Cyprus
Czechoslovakia
Denmark
Djibouti
Dominica
Dominican Republic
Ecuador
Egypt
El Salvador
Ethiopia
Fiji
Finland
France
Gabon

Gambia
German Democratic
 Republic
Germany, Federal Republic
 of
Ghana
Granada
Greece
Guatemala
Guinea-Bissau
Guyana
Haiti
Holy See
Honduras
Hungary
Iceland
India
Indonesia
Iran
Iraq
Ireland
Israel
Italy
Ivory Coast
Jamaica
Japan
Jordan
Kampuchea, Democratic
Kenya
Korea, Democratic People's
 Republic of
Korea, Republic of
Kuwait

Lao Republic
Lebanon
Lesotho
Liberia
Libya
Liechtenstein
Luxembourg
Madagascar
Malawi
Malaysia
Mali
Malta
Mauritania
Mauritius
Mexico
Monaco
Mongolia
Morocco
Nepal
Netherlands
New Zealand
Nicaragua
Niger
Nigeria
Norway
Oman
Pakistan
Panama
Papua New Guinea
Paraquay
Peru
Philippines
Poland

Portugal
Qatar
Romania
Rwanda
St. Lucia
St. Vincent and The
  Grenadines
San Marino
Sao Tome and Principe
Saudi Arabia
Senegal
Seychelles
Sierra Leone
Singapore
Somalia
South Africa
Spain
Sri Lanka
Sudan
Surinam
Swaziland
Sweden
Switzerland
Syrian Arab Republic

Tanzania
Thailand
Togo
Tonga
Trinidad and Tobago
Tunisia
Turkey
Tuvalu
Uganda
Ukrainian S.S.R.
U.S.S.R.
United Arab Emirates
United Kingdom
United States
Upper Volta
Uruguay
Venezuela
Vietnam
Yemen, Arab Republic
Yemen, Democratic
Yugoslavia
Zaire
Zambia

U.S. Action

Message from the President Transmitting the Geneva Conventions, S. Exec. Doc. D, E, F & G, 82d Cong., 1st Sess. (1951).

Geneva Conventions for the Protection of War Victims: Hearings Before the Senate Foreign Relations Comm., 84th Cong., 1st Sess. (1955).

Senate Comm. on Foreign Relations, Report on the Geneva Conventions for the Protection of War Victims, S. Exec. Rep. 9, 84th Cong., 1st Sess. (1955).

Cases

FEDERAL

Court of Appeals

Huynh Thi Anh v. Levi, 586 F.2d 625, 629 (6th Cir. 1978).

Nguyen Da Yen v. Kissinger, 528 F.2d 1194, 1201 n.13 (9th Cir. 1975).

United States v. Nat'l Comm. for Impeachment, 469 F.2d 1135, 1147 App. (2d Cir. 1972).

United States v. Owens, 415 F.2d 1308, 1315 (6th Cir. 1969), *cert. denied*, 397 U.S. 997 (1970).

District Court

Hanoch Tel-Oren v. Libyan Arab Republic, 517 F. Supp. 542, 546 (D.D.C. 1981).

United States v. Morales, 464 F. Supp. 325, 326 (E.D.N.Y. 1979).

United States v. Vargas, 370 F. Supp. 908, 917-20 (D.P.R. 1974), *rev'd and remanded on other grounds*, 558 F.2d 631 (1st Cir. 1977).

STATE

Hawaii

State v. Marley, 54 Hawaii 450, 464, 466 n.14, 509 P.2d 1095, 1105, 1106 n.14 (1973).

8. Universal Postal Convention, *signed* July 5, 1974, *entered into force* Jan. 1, 1976, 27 U.S.T. 345, T.I.A.S. No. 8231 (*entered into force* for U.S. Mar. 4, 1976).

Editor's Note

The General Postal Convention was signed by representatives of 22 States at the Congress of Berne of September 15, 1874. All 22 States ratified the Congress by the beginning of 1876 and the General Postal Union began operations that year. In 1878, the organization changed its name to the Universal Postal Union.

The Convention has been modified several times, including revisions at Paris in 1878 and 1947, at Ottawa in 1957 and Vienna in 1964. New Congresses are to take place every five years. Each successive Congress since the Berne Congress has had a final protocol, containing reservations to and derogations from provisions that are unacceptable to certain member States. The protocol as signed has the force and effect of the underlying Convention.

The most recent additional protocol was signed at Lausanne on July 5, 1974 and approved by the President on March 4, 1976. This protocol was the second additional protocol to the Constitution of the Universal Postal Union concluded at Vienna on July 10, 1964. 16 U.S.T. 1291, T.I.A.S. No. 5881 *entered into force* for U.S. July 10, 1964. *See also* the First Additional Protocol, done at Tokyo Nov. 14, 1969, *entered into force* for the U.S. July 1, 1971, with the exception of Article V which *entered into force* Jan. 1, 1971, 22 U.S.T. 1056, T.I.A.S. No. 7150.

Text of Chapter 1, Article 13(e) of the Convention

The Governments of member countries shall undertake to adopt, or to propose to the legislatures of their countries, the necessary measures: . . .

(e) for preventing and, if necessary, for punishing the insertion in postal items . . . explosive or easily inflammable substances where their insertion has not been expressly authorized by the Convention and the Agreements.

States Parties

(as of 1 March 1982)

Afghanistan
Albania
Algeria
Angola
Argentina
Australia
Austria
Bahamas
Bahrain
Bangladesh
Barbados
Belgium
Benin
Bhutan
Bolivia
Botswana
Brazil
Bulgaria
Burma
Burundi
Byelorussian S.S.R.
Cameroon
Canada
Cape Verde
Central African Republic
Chad

Chile
China, People's Republic of
Colombia
Comoros
Congo
Costa Rica
Cuba
Cyprus
Czechoslovakia
Denmark
Djibouti
Dominican Republic
Ecuador
Egypt
El Salvador
Equatorial Guinea
Ethiopia
Fiji
Finland
France
Gabon
Gambia Republic
German Democratic
   Republic
Germany, Federal Republic
   of

111

Ghana	Madagascar
Greece	Malawi
Granada	Malaysia
Guatemala	Maldives
Guinea	Mali
Guinea-Bissau	Mauritania
Guyana	Mauritius
Haiti	Mexico
Honduras	Monaco
Hungary	Mongolia
Iceland	Morocco
India	Mozambique
Indonesia	Nauru
Iran	Nepal
Iraq	Netherlands
Ireland	New Zealand
Israel	Nicaragua
Italy	Niger
Ivory Coast	Nigeria
Jamaica	Norway
Japan	Oman
Jordan	Pakistan
Kampuchea, Democratic	Panama
Kenya	Papua New Guinea
Korea, Republic of	Paraguay
Kuwait	Peru
Lao Republic	Philippines
Lebanon	Poland
Lesotho	Portugal
Liberia	Qatar
Libya	Romania
Liechtenstein	Rwanda
Luxembourg	St. Lucia

St. Vincent and the
  Grenadines
San Marino
Sao Tome and Principe
Saudi Arabia
Senegal
Seychelles
Sierra Leone
Singapore
Somalia
South Africa (expelled 11
  June 1981)
Spain
Sri Lanka
Sudan
Surinam
Swaziland
Sweden
Switzerland
Syrian Arab Republic
Tanzania
Thailand

Togo
Tonga
Trinidad and Tobago
Tunisia
Turkey
Tuvalu
Uganda
Ukrainian S.S.R.
U.S.S.R.
United Arab Emirates
United Kingdom
United States
Upper Volta
Uruguay
Vatican City
Venezuela
Vietnam
Yemen, Arab Republic
Yemen, Democratic
Yugoslavia
Zaire
Zambia

9. Convention on the Prevention and Punishment of the
   Crime of Genocide, *opened for signature* Dec. 9, 1948,
   entered into force Jan. 12, 1951, 78 U.N.T.S. 277.

Editor's Note

Occasionally, charges of genocide have been leveled by a
victim group or State against the authors of terrorist acts,
e.g., allegations of genocide and mass acts of terrorism by

Portugese troops in Mozambique and similar atrocities by Frelimo supporters against supporters of Portugal. *See* Green, The Nature and Control of International Terrorism 28 (Occasional Paper 1, Dep't of Political Science, University of Alberta, 1974).

The Convention makes genocide an international crime and commits the Contracting Parties to undertake to prevent and punish it (Article 2). Genocide is defined as the commission of certain acts with the intent to destroy, in whole or part, a national, ethnic, racial, or religious group, as such. The acts include killing, causing serious bodily or mental harm, deliberate infliction of conditions of life calculated to bring about physical destruction of a group, imposing birth control measures, and forcible transfer of children (Article 2). Acts that lead to or aid genocide, such as conspiracy, incitement, attempt and complicity, also are made criminal (Article 3).

The Convention provides that the "competent tribunal of the State in the territory of which the act was committed" has jurisdiction to try the offender (Article 6). An offender also may be tried by an international criminal court if one ever is established and the Contracting Parties have accepted its jurisdiction (Article 6).

Although States Parties to the Convention undertake to legislate against genocide (Article 5), the Convention does not give any State the right to prosecute alleged offenders merely because it has apprehended them. Instead, States are obligated to extradite offenders to the appropriate jurisdiction "in accordance with their laws and treaties in force" (Article 7). Genocide and other acts made criminal by Article 3 are not to be considered political offenses for extradition purposes (Article 7).

114

States Parties

(as of 1 March 1982)

Afghanistan
Albania
Algeria
Argentina
Australia
Austria
Bahamas
Barbados
Belgium
Brazil
Bulgaria
Burma
Byelorussian S.S.R.
Canada
Chile
China, Republic of
Colombia
Costa Rica
Cuba
Czechoslovakia
Denmark
Ecuador
Egypt
El Salvador
Ethiopia
Fiji
Finland
France
Gambia

German Democratic
  Republic
Germany, Federal Republic
  of
Ghana
Greece
Guatemala
Haiti
Honduras
Hungary
Iceland
India
Iran
Iraq
Ireland
Israel
Italy
Jamaica
Jordan
Kampuchea, Democratic
Korea, Republic of
Lao Republic
Lebanon
Lesotho
Liberia
Luxembourg
Mali
Mexico
Monaco

Mongolia
Morocco
Nepal
Netherlands
Nicaragua
Norway
Pakistan
Panama
Papua-New Guinea
Peru
Philippines
Poland
Romania
Rwanda
St. Vincent and the
  Grenadines
Saudi Arabia

Spain
Sri Lanka
Sweden
Syrian Arab Republic
Tonga
Tunisia
Turkey
Ukrainian S.S.R.
U.S.S.R.
United Kingdom
Upper Volta
Uruguay
Venezuela
Vietnam
Yugoslavia
Zaire

U.S. Action

Message from the President Transmitting the Genocide Convention, S. Exec. Doc. O, 81st Cong., 1st Sess. (1949).

Hearings Before a Subcomm. of the Senate Foreign Relations Comm. on Exec. O, 81st Cong., 1st Sess., 2d Sess. (1950).

Renewal of Request for Consent to Ratification of the International Convention on the Prevention and Punishment of the Crime of Genocide (Exec. O, 81st Cong., 1st Sess.), Exec. Rep. B, 91st Cong., 2d Sess. (1970).

Hearings Before a Subcomm. of the Senate Foreign Relations Comm. on Exec. O, 81st Cong., 1st Sess.; 91st Cong., 2d Sess. (1970).

Senate Comm. on Foreign Relations, Report on the International Convention on the Prevention and Punishment of the Crime of Genocide, S. Exec. Rep. 25, 91st Cong., 2d Sess. (1970).

Hearing Before a Subcomm. of the Senate Foreign Relations Comm. on Exec. O, 81st Cong., 1st Sess.; 92d Cong., 1st Sess. (1971).

Senate Comm. on Foreign Relations, Report on the International Convention on the Prevention and Punishment of the Crime of Genocide, S. Exec. Rep. 6, 92d Cong., 1st Sess. (1971).

Senate Comm. on Foreign Relations, Report on the International Convention on the Prevention and Punishment of the Crime of Genocide, S. Exec. Rep. 5, 93d Cong., 1st Sess. (1973).

Senate Comm. on Foreign Relations, Report on the International Convention on the Prevention and Punishment of the Crime of Genocide, S. Exec. Rep. 23, 94th Cong., 1st Sess. (1976).

Hearings Before the Subcomm. on Future Foreign Policy Research and Development, Investigation Into Certain Past Instances of Genocide and Exploration of Policy Options for the Future, 94th Cong., 2d Sess. (1976).

Hearings Before the Senate Comm. on Foreign Relations on Exec. O, 81st Cong., 1st Sess.; 95th Cong., 1st Sess. (1977).

Cases

FEDERAL

Court of Appeals

Jewish War Veterans of United States v. American Nazi Party, 260 F. Supp. 452, 454 (N.D. Ill. 1966).

Hanoch Tel-Oren v. Libyan Arab Republic, 517 F. Supp. 542, 546 (D.D.C. 1981).

STATE

New York

Byrn v. New York City Health & Hosps. Corp., 31 N.Y.2d 194, 208, 209, 286 N.E.2d 887, 893, 894, 335 N.Y.S.2d 390, 399 (1972) (Burke, J., dissenting).

10. Convention on the Non-Applicability of Statutory Limitations to War Crimes and Crimes Against Humanity, *adopted* Nov. 26, 1968, *entered into force* Nov. 11, 1970, 754 U.N.T.S. 73.

Editor's Note

The Convention provides that no statutory limitation shall apply to the following crimes, *inter alia,* irrespective of the date of their commission: (1) war crimes as they are defined in the Charter of the International Military Tribunal, Nuremberg, of 8 August 1945, particularly the "grave breaches" enumerated in the Geneva Conventions of 12 August 1949 for the protection of war victims; and (2) crimes against humanity, whether committed in time of war or in time of peace as they are defined in the Charter of the Military Tribunal, Nuremberg of 8 August 1945, including the crime of genocide as defined in the 1948 Convention on the Prevention and Punishment of Genocide (Article 1).

The Convention commits the Contracting States to "undertake to adopt all necessary domestic measures, legislative or otherwise," with a view to making possible extradition of persons who, "as principals or accomplices, participate in or who directly incite others to the commission" of any of the above crimes, or who conspire to commit them and of "representatives of the State authority who tolerate their commission" (Articles 2 & 3).

States Parties

(as of 1 March 1982)

Albania
Bulgaria
Byelorussian S.S.R.
Cameroon
Cuba
Czechoslovakia
Gambia
German Democratic Republic
Guinea
Hungary
India
Kenya
Mongolia
Nigeria
Philippines
Poland
Romania
Rwanda
St. Vincent and the
   Grenadines
Tunisia
Ukrainian S.S.R.
U.S.S.R.
Yugoslavia

B. European Conventions

1. European Convention on the Suppression of Terrorism, *signed* Jan. 27, 1977, *entered into force* Aug. 4, 1978, (Cmd. 7031), *reprinted in* 15 Int'l Legal Materials 1272 (1976).

Editor's Note

The Convention outlines offenses which for purposes of extradition will not be regarded as political offenses: attacks upon internationally protected persons, kidnapping and hostage taking, offenses endangering persons involving the use of a bomb, and offenses under the Hague and Montreal Conventions (Article 1). A Contracting State also may choose not to regard as political offenses actions involving other forms of violence (Article 2). The Convention supersedes all extradition and mutual assistance treaties between Contracting States to the extent that they are incompatible with it (Articles 3 & 8).

A Contracting State is obligated under Article 7 to prosecute any person whom it refuses to extradite. However, if the requested state has "substantial grounds" for believing that the purpose of the extradition would be to prosecute or punish a person on account of his race, religion, nationality or political opinion, the state is under no obligation to afford assistance (Article 8). Article 9 provides that the European Committee on Crime Problems of the Council of Europe, which "shall be kept informed regarding the application of this convention," shall do whatever is needed "to facilitate a friendly settlement of any difficulty which may arise out of its execution." If a resolution is unobtainable, the dispute is to be referred to arbitration (Article 10).

The Convention is open to all member States of the Council of Europe. Article 13 allows a State to reserve the right to refuse extradition in respect to offenses it considers to be political or inspired by political motives, though it must make such a reservation at the time of signature or when depositing its instrument of ratification, acceptance or approval. *The Agreement Concerning the Application of the European Convention on the Suppression of Terrorism Among the Member States* (which immediately follows this Convention) outlines the relations between member States of which at least one is not a party to the Convention, or is a party to the Convention but with a reservation.

Text of the Convention

The member States of the Council of Europe, signatory hereto,

Considering that the aim of the Council of Europe is to achieve a greater unity between its Members;

Aware of the growing concern caused by the increase in acts of terrorism;

Wishing to take effective measures to ensure that the perpetrators of such acts do not escape prosecution and punishment;

Convinced that extradition is a particularly effective measure for achieving this result;

Have agreed as follows:

ARTICLE 1

For the purposes of extradition between Contracting States, none of the following offences shall be regarded as a political offence or as an offence connected with a political offence or as an offence inspired by political motives:

(a) an offence within the scope of the Convention for the Suppression of Unlawful Seizure of Aircraft, signed at The Hague on 16 December 1970;

(b) an offence within the scope of the Convention for the Suppression of Unlawful Acts against the Safety of Civil Aviation, signed at Montreal on 23 September 1971;

(c) a serious offence involving an attack against the life, physical integrity or liberty of internationally protected persons, including diplomatic agents;

(d) an offence involving kidnapping, the taking of a hostage or serious unlawful detention;

(e) an offence involving the use of a bomb, grenade, rocket, automatic firearm or letter or parcel bomb if this use endangers persons;

(f) an attempt to commit any of the foregoing offences or participation as an accomplice of a person who commits or attempts to commit such an offence.

ARTICLE 2

1. For the purposes of extradition between Contracting States, a Contracting State may decide not to regard as a political offence or as an offence connected with a political offence or as an offence inspired by political motives a serious offence involving an act of violence, other than one covered by Article 1, against the life, physical integrity or liberty of a person.

2. The same shall apply to a serious offence involving an act against property, other than one covered by Article 1, if the act created a collective danger for persons.

3. The same shall apply to an attempt to commit any of the foregoing offences or participation as an accomplice of a person who commits or attempts to commit such an offence.

ARTICLE 3

The provisions of all extradition treaties and arrangements applicable between Contracting States, including the European Convention on Extradition, are modified as between Contracting States to the extent that they are incompatible with this Convention.

ARTICLE 4

For the purposes of this Convention and to the extent that any offence mentioned in Article 1 or 2 is not listed as an extraditable offence in any extradition convention or treaty existing between Contracting States, it shall be deemed to be included as such therein.

ARTICLE 5

Nothing in this Convention shall be interpreted as imposing an obligation to extradite if the requested State has substantial grounds for believing that the request for extradition for an offence mentioned in Article 1 or 2 has been made for the purpose of prosecuting or punishing a person on account of his race, religion, nationality or political opinion, or that that person's position may be prejudiced for any of these reasons.

ARTICLE 6

1. Each Contracting State shall take such measures as may be necessary to establish its jurisdiction over an offence mentioned in Article 1 in the case where the suspected offender is present in its territory and it does not extradite him after receiving a request for extradition from a Contracting State whose jurisdiction is based on a rule of jurisdiction existing equally in the law of the requested State.

2. This convention does not exclude any criminal jurisdiction exercised in accordance with national law.

ARTICLE 7

A Contracting State in whose territory a person suspected to have committed an offence mentioned in Article 1 is found and which has received a request for extradition under the conditions mentioned in Article 6, paragraph 1, shall, if it does not extradite that person, submit the case, without exception whatsoever and without undue delay, to its competent authorities for the purpose of prosecution. Those authorities shall take their decision in the same manner as in the case of any offence of a serious nature under the law of that State.

ARTICLE 8

1. Contracting States shall afford one another the widest measure of mutual assistance in criminal matters in connection with proceedings brought in respect of the offences mentioned in Article 1 or 2. The law of the requested State concerning mutual assistance in criminal matters shall apply in all cases. Nevertheless this assistance may not be refused on the sole ground that it concerns a political offence or an offence connected with a political offence or an offence inspired by political motives.

2. Nothing in this Convention shall be interpreted as imposing an obligation to afford mutual assistance if the requested State has substantial grounds for believing that the request for mutual assistance in respect of an offence mentioned in Article 1 or 2 has been made for the purpose of prosecuting or punishing a person on account of his race, religion, nationality or political opinion or that that person's position may be prejudiced for any of these reasons.

124

3. The provisions of all treaties and arrangements concerning mutual assistance in criminal matters applicable between Contracting States, including the European Convention on Mutual Assistance in Criminal Matters, are modified as between Contracting States to the extent that they are incompatible with this Convention.

ARTICLE 9

1. The European Committee on Crime Problems of the Council of Europe shall be kept informed regarding the application of this Convention.

2. It shall do whatever is needful to facilitate a friendly settlement of any difficulty which may arise out of its execution.

ARTICLE 10

1. Any dispute between Contracting States concerning the interpretation or application of this Convention, which has not been settled in the framework of Article 9, paragraph 2, shall, at the request of any Party to the dispute, be referred to arbitration. Each Party shall nominate an arbitrator and the two arbitrators shall nominate a referee. If any Party has not nominated its arbitrator within the three months following the request for arbitration, he shall be nominated at the request of the other Party by the President of the European Court of Human Rights. If the latter should be a national of one of the Parties to the dispute, this duty shall be carried out by the Vice-President of the Court, or, if the Vice-President is a national of one of the Parties to the dispute, by the most senior judge of the Court not being a national of one of the Parties to the dispute. The same procedure shall be observed if the arbitrators cannot agree on the choice of referee.

2. The arbitration tribunal shall lay down its own procedure. Its decisions shall be taken by majority vote. Its award shall be final.

ARTICLE 11

1. This Convention shall be open to signature by the member States of the Council of Europe. It shall be subject to ratification, acceptance or approval. Instruments of ratification, acceptance or approval shall be deposited with the Secretary-General of the Council of Europe.

2. The Convention shall enter into force three months after the date of the deposit of the third instrument of ratification, acceptance or approval.

3. In respect of a signatory State ratifying, accepting or approving subsequently, the Convention shall come into force three months after the date of the deposit of its instrument of ratification, acceptance or approval.

ARTICLE 12

1. Any State may, at the time of signature or when depositing its instrument of ratification, acceptance or approval, specify the territory or territories to which this Convention shall apply.

2. Any State may, when depositing its instrument of ratification, acceptance or approval or at any later date, by declaration addressed to the Secretary-General of the Council of Europe, extend this Convention to any other territory or territories specified in the declaration and for whose international relations it is responsible or on whose behalf it is authorized to give undertakings.

3. Any declaration made in pursuance of the preceding paragraph may, in respect of any territory mentioned in such declaration, be withdrawn by means of a notification

addressed to the Secretary-General of the Council of Europe. Such withdrawal shall take effect immediately or at such later date as may be specified in the notification.

ARTICLE 13

1. Any State may, at the time of signature or when depositing its instrument of ratification, acceptance or approval, declare that it reserves the right to refuse extradition in respect of any offence mentioned in Article 1 which it considers to be a political offence, an offence connected with a political offence or an offence inspired by political motives, provided that it undertakes to take into due consideration, when evaluating the character of the offence, any particularly serious aspects of the offence, including:

(a) that it created a collective danger to the life, physical integrity or liberty of persons; or

(b) that it affected persons foreign to the motives behind it; or

(c) that cruel or vicious means have been used in the commission of the offence.

2. Any State may wholly or partly withdraw a reservation it has made in accordance with the foregoing paragraph by means of a declaration addressed to the Secretary-General of the Council of Europe which shall become effective as from the date of its receipt.

3. A State which has made a reservation in accordance with paragraph 1 of this article may not claim the application of Article 1 by any other State; it may, however, if its reservation is partial or conditional, claim the application of that article in so far as it has itself accepted it.

ARTICLE 14

Any Contracting State may denounce this Convention by means of a written notification addressed to the Secretary-General of the Council of Europe. Any such denunciation shall take effect immediately or at such later date as may be specified in the notification.

ARTICLE 15

This Convention ceases to have effect in respect of any Contracting State which withdraws from or ceases to be a Member of the Council of Europe.

ARTICLE 16

The Secretary-General of the Council of Europe shall notify the member States of the Council of:

(a) any signature;

(b) any deposit of an instrument of ratification, acceptance or approval;

(c) any date of entry into force of this Convention in accordance with Article 11 thereof;

(d) any declaration or notification received in pursuance of the provisions of Article 12;

(e) any reservation made in pursuance of the provisions of Article 13, paragraph 1;

(f) the withdrawal of any reservation effected in pursuance of the provisions of Article 13, paragraph 2;

(g) any notification received in pursuance of Article 14 and the date on which denunciation takes effect;

(h) any cessation of the effects of the Convention pursuant to Article 15.

CONVENTIONS PROSCRIBING TERRORIST ACTS

States Parties

(as of 1 March 1982)

Austria
Cyprus
Denmark
Germany, Federal Republic of
Liechtenstein
Norway
Sweden
United Kingdom

2. Agreement Concerning the Application of the European
   Convention on the Suppression of Terrorism among the
   Member States, *done* at Dublin, Dec. 4, 1979, *reprinted
   in* 12 Bulletin of the European Communities No. 12, at
   90-91 (1979).

Editor's Note

This Agreement outlines the minimum obligations of
member States of the European Community. Where one of
the member States is not bound by the European Convention on the Suppression of Terrorism, or is bound but has
reserved rights under the Convention, the Agreement
identified the obligations a member State owes to other
member States. The Agreement was signed by the Minister
of Justice of the nine member States of the Community. The
Agreement ceases to have effect when all the Member
States become parties without reservation to the European
Convention.

Text of the Agreement

Agreement concerning the application of the European Convention on the Suppression of Terrorism among the Member States of the European Communities

The Member States of the European Communities,

Concerned to strengthen judicial cooperation among these States in the fight against acts of violence,

While awaiting the ratification without reservations of the European Convention on the Suppression of Terrorism signed at Strasbourg on 27 January 1977, described below as "the European Convention", by all the Member States of the European Communities, described below as "the Member States",

Have agreed as follows:

ARTICLE 1

This Agreement shall apply in relations between two Member States of which one at least is not a party to the European Convention or is a party to that Convention, but with a reservation.

ARTICLE 2

1. In the relations between two Member States which are parties to the European Convention, but of which one at least has made a reservation to that Convention, the application of the said Convention shall be subject to the provisions of this Agreement.

2. In the relations between two Member States of which one at least is not a party to the European Convention, Articles 1 to 8 and 13 of that Convention shall apply subject to the provisions of this Agreement.

ARTICLE 3

1. Each Member State which has made the reservation permitted under Article 13 of the European Convention shall declare whether, for the application of this Agreement, it intends to make use of this reservation.

2. Each Member State which has signed the European Convention but has not ratified, accepted or approved it, shall declare whether, for the application of this Agreement, it intends to make the reservation permitted under Article 13 of that Convention.

3. Each Member State which has not signed the European Convention may declare that it reserves the right to refuse extradition for an offence listed in Article 1 of that Convention which it considers to be a political offence, an offence connected with a political offence or an offence inspired by political motives, on condition that it undertakes to submit the case without exception whatsoever and without undue delay, to its competent authorities for the purpose of prosecution. Those authorities shall take their decision in the same manner as in the case of any offence of a serious nature under the law of that State.

4. For the application of this Agreement, only the reservations provided for in paragraph 3 of this Article and in Article 13 of the European Convention are permitted. Any other reservation is without effect as between the Member States.

5. A Member State which has made a reservation may only claim the application of this Agreement by another State to the extent that the Agreement itself applies to the former State.

ARTICLE 4

1. The declarations provided for under Article 3 may be made by a Member State at the time of signature or when depositing its instrument of ratification, acceptance or approval.

2. Each Member State may at any time, wholly or partially, withdraw a reservation which it has made in pursuance of paragraphs 1, 2 or 3 of Article 3 by means of a declaration addressed to the Department of Foreign Affairs of Ireland. The declaration shall have effect on the day it is received.

3. The Department of Foreign Affairs of Ireland shall communicate the declarations to the other Member States.

ARTICLE 5

Any dispute between Member States concerning the interpretation or application of this Agreement which has not been settled by negotiation shall, at the request of any party to the dispute, be referred to arbitration in accordance with the procedure laid down in Article 10 of the European Convention.

ARTICLE 6

1. This Agreement shall be open for signature by the Member States of the European Communities. It shall be subject to ratification, acceptance or approval. Instruments of ratification, acceptance or approval shall be deposited with the Department of Foreign Affairs of Ireland.

2. The Agreement shall enter into force three months after the deposit of the instruments of ratification, acceptance or approval by all States which are members of the European Communities on the day on which this Agreement is opened for signature.

ARTICLE 7

1. Each Member State may, at the time of signature or when depositing its instrument of ratification, acceptance or approval, specify the territory or territories to which this Agreement shall apply.

2. Each Member State may, when depositing its instrument of ratification, acceptance or approval or at any later date, by declaration addressed to the Department of Foreign Affairs of Ireland extend this Agreement to any other territory specified in the declaration and for whose international relations it is responsible or on whose behalf it is authorized to give undertakings.

3. Any declaration made in pursuance of the preceding paragraph may, as regards any territory specified in that declaration, be denounced by means of a notification addressed to the Department of Foreign Affairs of Ireland. The denunciation shall have effect immediately or at such later date as may be specified in the notification.

4. The Department of Foreign Affairs of Ireland shall communicate these declarations and notifications to the other Member States.

ARTICLE 8

This Agreement shall cease to have effect on the date when all the Member States become parties without reservation to the European Convention.

States Parties

(as of 1 March 1982)

Belgium
Denmark

France
Germany, Federal Republic of
Ireland
Italy
Luxembourg
Netherlands
United Kingdom

C. Physical Protection of Nuclear Material

1. Convention on the Physical Protection of Nuclear Material, *concluded* Oct. 26, 1979, *opened for signature* Mar. 3, 1980, *reprinted in* 18 Int'l Legal Materials 1419 (1979).

Editor's Note

The Convention on the Physical Protection of Nuclear Material was negotiated between fifty-eight States and one organization (the European Atomic Energy Commission) under the aegis of the International Atomic Energy Commission (IAEA). It will enter into force after the twenty-first State ratifies it; ratifications are to be deposited with the IAEA.

The Convention establishes standards for the protection of nuclear material during international transport. It requires States-parties to provide for the punishment of persons who commit any of an enumerated series of offenses involving nuclear material (Article 7). These offenses are deemed to be extraditable offenses (Article 11) and States have an obligation to prosecute or extradite alleged offenders (Articles 9 and 10).

134

Article 8 requires a Contracting State to extend by national legislation its jurisdiction over the offenses enumerated in Article 7 to all ships and aircraft registered in that State and to all nationals of that State. Contracting States must cooperate in preventive measures (Article 5) and in the exchange of information and evidence needed in criminal proceedings (Article 13).

The European Court of Justice ruled that members of the European Atomic Energy Commission could subject themselves to the provisions of this Convention only to the extent that "the Community as such is a party to the convention on the same lines as the states." Ruling 1/78, 1978 E. Comm. Ct. J. Rep. 2151, 2181, [1979] C.M.L.R. 131.

Selected Articles of the Convention

THE STATES PARTIES TO THIS CONVENTION,

RECOGNIZING the right of all States to develop and apply nuclear energy for peaceful purposes and their legitimate interests in the potential benefits to be derived from the peaceful application of nuclear energy,

CONVINCED of the need for facilitating international co-operation in the peaceful application of nuclear energy,

DESIRING to avert the potential dangers posed by the unlawful taking and use of nuclear material,

CONVINCED that offences relating to nuclear material are a matter of grave concern and that there is an urgent need to adopt appropriate and effective measures to ensure the prevention, detection and punishment of such offences,

AWARE OF THE NEED FOR international co-operation to establish, in conformity with the national law of each State Party and with this Convention, effective measures for the physical protection of nuclear material,

135

CONVINCED that this Convention should facilitate the safe transfer of nuclear material,

STRESSING also the importance of the physical protection of nuclear material in domestic use, storage and transport,

RECOGNIZING the importance of effective physical protection of nuclear material used for military purposes, and understanding that such material is and will continue to be accorded stringent physical protection,

HAVE AGREED as follows:

* * *

Article 5

1. States Parties shall identify and make known to each other directly or through the International Atomic Energy Agency their central authority and point of contact having responsibility for physical protection of nuclear material and for co-ordinating recovery and response operations in the event of any unauthorized removal, use or alteration of nuclear material or in the event of credible threat thereof.

2. In the case of theft, robbery or any other unlawful taking of nuclear material or of credible threat thereof, States Parties shall, in accordance with their national law, provide co-operation and assistance to the maximum feasible extent in the recovery and protection of such material to any State that so requests. In particular:

(a) a State Party shall take appropriate steps to inform as soon as possible other States, which appear to it to be concerned, of any theft, robbery or other unlawful taking of nuclear material or credible threat thereof and to inform, where appropriate, international organizations;

(b) as appropriate, the States Parties concerned shall exchange information with each other or international organizations with a view to protecting threatened nuclear material, verifying the integrity of the shipping container, or recovering unlawfully taken nuclear material and shall:

(i) co-ordinate their efforts through diplomatic and other agreed channels;

(ii) render assistance, if requested;

(iii) ensure the return of nuclear material stolen or missing as a consequence of the above-mentioned events.

The means of implementation of this co-operation shall be determined by the States Parties concerned.

3. States Parties shall co-operate and consult as appropriate, with each other directly or through international organizations, with a view to obtaining guidance on the design, maintenance and improvement of systems of physical protection of nuclear material in international transport.

ARTICLE 6

1. States Parties shall take appropriate measures consistent with their national law to protect the confidentiality of any information which they receive in confidence by virtue of the provisions of this Convention from another State Party or through participation in an activity carried out for the implementation of this Convention. If States Parties provide information to international organizations in confidence, steps shall be taken to ensure that the confidentiality of such information is protected.

2. States Parties shall not be required by this Convention to provide any information which they are not permitted to communicate pursuant to national law or which would jeopardize the security of the State concerned or the physical protection of nuclear material.

ARTICLE 7

1. The intentional commission of:

(a) an act without lawful authority which constitutes the receipt, possession, use, transfer, alteration, disposal or dispersal of nuclear material and which causes or is likely to cause death or serious injury to any person or substantial damage to property;

(b) a theft or robbery of nuclear material;

(c) an embezzlement or fraudulent obtaining of nuclear material;

(d) an act constituting a demand for nuclear material by threat or use of force or by any other form of intimidation;

(e) a threat:

(i) to use nuclear material to cause death or serious injury to any person or substantial property damage, or

(ii) to commit an offence described in sub-paragraph (b) in order to compel a natural or legal person, international organization or State to do or to refrain from doing any act;

(f) an attempt to commit any offence described in paragraphs (a), (b) or (c); and

(g) an act which constitutes participation in any offence described in paragraphs (a) to (f)

shall be made a punishable offence by each State Party under its national law.

2. Each State Party shall make the offences described in this article punishable by appropriate penalties which take into account their grave nature.

ARTICLE 8

1. Each State Party shall take such measures as may be necessary to establish its jurisdiction over the offences set forth in article 7 in the following cases:

(a) when the offence is committed in the territory of that State or on board a ship or aircraft registered in that State;

(b) when the alleged offender is a national of that State.

2. Each State Party shall likewise take such measures as may be necessary to establish its jurisdiction over these offences in cases where the alleged offender is present in its territory and it does not extradite him pursuant to article 11 to any of the States mentioned in paragraph 1.

3. This Convention does not exclude any criminal jurisdiction exercised in accordance with national law.

4. In addition to the States Parties mentioned in paragraphs 1 and 2, each State Party may, consistent with international law, establish its jurisdiction over the offences set forth in article 7 when it is involved in international nuclear transport as the exporting or importing State.

ARTICLE 9

Upon being satisfied that the circumstances so warrant, the State Party in whose territory the alleged offender is present shall take appropriate measures, including detention, under its national law to ensure his presence for the purpose of prosecution or extradition. Measures taken according to this article shall be notified without delay to the States required to establish jurisdiction pursuant to article 8 and, where appropriate, all other States concerned.

ARTICLE 10

The State Party in whose territory the alleged offender is present shall, if it does not extradite him, submit, without exception whatsoever and without undue delay, the case to its competent authorities for the purpose of prosecution, through proceedings in accordance with the laws of that State.

ARTICLE 11

1. The offences in article 7 shall be deemed to be included as extraditable offences in any extradition treaty existing between States Parties. States Parties undertake to include those offences as extraditable offences in every future extradition treaty to be concluded between them.

2. If a State Party which make extradition conditional on the existence of a treaty receives a request for extradition from another State Party with which it has no extradition treaty, it may at its option consider this Convention as the legal basis for extradition in respect of those offences. Extradition shall be subject to the other conditions provided by the law of the requested State.

3. States Parties which do not make extradition conditional on the existence of a treaty shall recognize those offences as extraditable offences between themselves subject to the conditions provided by the law of the requested State.

4. Each of the offences shall be treated, for the purpose of extradition between States Parties, as if it had been committed not only in the place in which it occurred but also in the territories of the States Parties required to establish their jurisdiction in accordance with paragraph 1 of article 8.

* * *

States Parties

(as of 1 March 1982)

(21 ratifications necessary for entry into force)

German Democratic Republic
Philippines
Sweden

U.S. Action

The Convention of the Physical Protection of Nuclear Material: Hearings Before the Senate Comm. on Foreign Relations, 97th Cong., 1st Sess. (1981).

II. MULTILATERAL EXTRADITION TREATIES AND AGREEMENTS

A. European Conventions on Extradition

1. European Convention on Extradition, *done* Dec. 13, 1957, *entered into force* Apr. 18, 1960, Europ. T.S. No. 24, 359 U.N.T.S. 273.

Editor's Note

The Convention aims to establish uniform rules respecting extradition among members of the Council of Europe. The Contracting States undertake to grant extradition in respect to offenses punishable under the laws of both the requesting and requested States by imprisonment for a period of at least one year or by a more severe penalty (Article 2). In the case of conviction in the

141

requesting State, the punishment awarded must have been for a period of at least four months (Article 2). The extradition of a State's own nationals is discretionary (Article 6).

Requests for provisional arrest may be channeled through the International Criminal Police Organization (Interpol) (Article 16).

Political offenses, the determination of which is left to the discretion of the requested State, are excluded from the category of extraditable crimes. The Convention, however, contains a *Belgian* clause, *i.e.,* the taking or attempted taking of the life of a Head of State or a member of his family is not to be deemed a political offense (Article 3).

The Convention is open to accession by non-members of the Council of Europe, provided the unanimous consent of those States which have ratified the Convention is obtained.

On 24 January 1972, the Committee of Ministers of the Council of Europe adopted a Resolution expressing, *inter alia,* its conviction "that the political motive alleged by the authors of certain acts of terrorism should not have as a result that they are neither extradited nor punished." When applying the European Convention on Extradition, as well as conventions and agreements dealing with terrorist acts, in respect to a request for extradition, States are urged to take into consideration the particularly serious nature of the terrorist acts. The resolution recommends that if extradition is refused "and if its jurisdiction rules permit, the government of the requested State should submit the case to its competent authorities for the purpose of prosecution." Further, it recommends that States lacking jurisdiction to try accused persons "should envisage the possibility of establishing it." (Res. 74[3] adopted by the Council of Europe, Committee of Ministers at its 53d Session, *Eur. Ass. Doc.,* 25th Sess., Doc. No. 3425, at 16.)

The Convention has been superseded, insofar as it governs extradition for acts of terrorism, by the European Convention on the Suppression of Terrorism. According to Article 3 of the latter, this Convention and "all extradition treaties and arrangements applicable between Contracting States" are modified to the extent that they are incompatible with the European Convention.

States Parties

(as of 1 March 1982)

Austria
Cyprus
Denmark
Finland
Germany, Federal Republic of
Greece
Ireland
Israel
Italy
Liechtenstein
Luxembourg
Netherlands
Norway
Portugal
Sweden
Switzerland
Turkey

Cases

FEDERAL
District Court
Sindona v. Grant, 619 F.2d 167, 177 (2d Cir. 1980).

2. Additional Protocol to the European Convention on Extradition, *adopted* Oct. 15, 1975, Europ. T.S. No. 86.

Editor's Note

The Protocol supplements the provisions of the 1957 Convention, particularly Articles 3 and 9. Article 1 of the Protocol specifies additional exclusions to the political offense exception to extradition. For purposes of Article 3 of the 1957 Convention, the following shall not be deemed political offenses:

(a) The crimes against humanity specified in the Convention on the Prevention and Punishment of the Crime of Genocide . . . ;

(b) The violations specified in Article 50 of the 1949 Geneva Convention for the Amelioration of the Condition of the Wounded and Sick in Armed Forces in the Field, Article 51 of the 1949 Geneva Convention for the Amelioration of the Condition of the Wounded, Sick and Shipwrecked Members of Armed Forces at Sea, Article 130 of the 1949 Geneva Convention relative to the Treatment of Prisoners of War and Article 147 of the 1949 Geneva Convention relative to the Protection of Civilian Persons in Time of War; [and]

(c) Any comparable violations of the laws of war having effect at the time when this Protocol enters into force and of customs of war existing at that time, which are not already provided for in the above-mentioned provisions of the Geneva Conventions.

The Protocol, like the European Convention on Extradition, has been superseded, insofar as it governs extradition for acts of terrorism, by the European Convention on the Suppression of Terrorism.

States Parties

(as of 1 March 1982)

Cyprus
Denmark
Sweden

3. Second Additional Protocol to the European Convention on Extradition, *done* Mar. 17, 1978, Europ. T.S. No. 98.

Editor's Note

The Second Additional Protocol, which enters into force upon ratification by at least three members of the Council of Europe who also have ratified the 1957 Convention, supplements Articles 2, 5 and 12 of the Convention. It extends the right for extradition to offenses in connection with taxes, duties, customs and exchange regulations, and adds provisions for judgments in absentia and for offenses in respect of which an amnesty has been declared in the requested country. The Protocol, not yet in force, must be read against the European Convention on the Suppression of Terrorism.

States Parties

(as of 1 March 1982)

Sweden

B. Inter-American Conventions on Extradition
Editor's Introductory Note

Numerous treaties and agreements concerning extradition have been concluded within the Inter-American system. Many of their provisions are overlapping. Together they create a "fairly cohesive and consistent development of principle," though the exact status of the States Parties in any particular extradition matter has to be assessed on the "chequer board" of the bilateral and multilateral treaties. (I. Shearer, *Extradition in International Law* 63 (1971).

1. Treaty for Extradition of Criminals and for Protection Against Anarchism, *adopted* Jan. 28, 1902, 6 *Martens Nouveau Recueil* (ser. 3) 185 (1941).

Editor's Note

The Treaty establishes the duty to extradite persons accused or sentenced by authorities of the Contracting Parties. Political offenders are exempted from extradition, except in cases involving acts of anarchism (Article 2). Extradition by a State of its own nationals is discretionary. This treaty never entered into force due to an insufficient number of ratifications.

States Parties

(as of 1 March 1982)

Costa Rica
El Salvador
Guatemala
Mexico

2. Code of Private International Law (Bustamente Code), *signed* Feb. 20, 1928, *entered into force* Nov. 26, 1928, 86 L.N.T.S. 111.

Editor's Note

The Code obliges Contracting States to extradite individuals accused or convicted of an offense punishable by one year imprisonment or a heavier penalty (Articles 344 & 354). Political offenses and acts related thereto are excluded from extradition (Article 355); homicide or murder of the head of a Contracting State, or of any other person exercising authority in that State, shall not be deemed a political offense (Article 357). While Contracting States are not obliged to extradite their own nationals, a State refusing to do so is obliged to prosecute the individual in question.

States Parties

(as of 1 March 1982)

Bolivia
Brazil
Chile
Costa Rica
Cuba
Dominican Republic
Ecuador
El Salvador
Guatemala
Haiti
Honduras
Nicaragua

Panama
Peru
Venezuela

3. 1933 Convention on Extradition, *signed* Dec. 26, 1933, *entered into force* Jan. 25, 1935, 49 Stat. 3111 (1935), T.S. No. 95, 165 L.N.T.S. 45 (*entered into force* for U.S. July 13, 1934).

Editor's Note

The Convention obligates Contracting States to extradite individuals accused or convicted of offenses punishable in both the requesting and requested States by a minimum penalty of one year's imprisonment. A State refusing to extradite one of its own nationals is obligated to submit his case to its appropriate authorities for prosecution.

The Convention contains a standard *Belgian* clause, *i.e.,* "[a]n attempt against the life or person of the Chief of State or members of his family, shall not be deemed to be a political offense . . . ." (Article 3).

The Convention does not abrogate or modify any prior existing agreements or treaties on the same subject which are in force between signatory States. The Convention, however, enters into force in the event of the lapse of the relevant portions of those prior treaties.

States Parties

(as of 1 March 1982)

Argentina
Chile

148

Columbia
Dominican Republic
Ecuador
El Salvador
Guatemala
Honduras
Mexico
Nicaragua
Panama
United States

4. Central American Convention on Extradition, *concluded* Dec. 20, 1907, 2 Malloy 2406 (1910).

Editor's Note

The Convention obligates States Parties to extradite individuals convicted or accused of offenses punishable under the laws of the requesting State by two years' imprisonment or by a heavier penalty (Article 1). Political offenses are excluded from extradition (Article 2). The Convention contains a standard *Belgian* clause, *i.e.,* attempts against the life of the Head of the Government or public functionaries are not to be considered political offenses. While the Contracting States are not obliged to deliver up their own nationals, they must try them for any offenses committed in another Contracting State (Article 4). This Convention is not in force and is mentioned here only for its historical importance.

States Parties

(as of 1 March 1982)

Nicaragua

5. Inter-American Convention on Extradition, *done* at Caracas, Feb. 25, 1981, O.A.S. Doc. OEA/Ser.A/36 (SEPF).

Editor's Note

The Convention obligates States Parties to extradite persons who are to be prosecuted, are being tried, have been convicted, or have been sentenced by another State Party (Article 1). For extradition to be granted the offense for which the person is sought must be punishable by at least two years' imprisonment in both the requesting and the requested States (Article 3). The requested State may deny extradition when it is competent, according to its own legislation, to prosecute the person whose extradition is sought (Article 2). Extradition may be denied as well for political offenses or when the tribunal to try or sentence the person sought is an extraordinary or *ad hoc* one (Article 4). The States Parties are precluded from granting extradition when an offense in question is punishable in the requesting State by the death penalty, life imprisonment or degrading punishment, unless the requested State has acquired assurances that none of those punishments will be enforced (Article 9).

The Convention does not relieve States Parties of their obligations under other bilateral or multilateral extradition agreements.

Signatories

(as of 1 March 1982)

Chile
Costa Rica
Dominican Republic
Ecuador
El Salvador
Guatemala
Haiti
Nicaragua
Panama
Uruguay
Venezuela

C. General

1. Benelux Convention on Extradition and Judicial Assistance in Penal Matters, *done* June 27, 1962, [1962] Trb. nr. 97, at 1-10, Benelux Publicatieblad 22 (1960-62).

Editor's Note

The Convention follows closely the European Convention on Extradition with several relevant exceptions: (1) the punishments sufficient to render an offense extraditable is six months' imprisonment for accused offenders and three months' for convicted fugitives, as compared to twelve and four months' imprisonment respectively under the European Convention; and (2) the extradition of a requested State's own nationals is not permitted (Articles 2 & 5).

The Convention excludes political offenses from extradition, but also contains a *Belgian* clause, *i.e.*, that the

151

attempt at the life or the freedom of a Head of State or of a member of the reigning House is not to be regarded as political (Article 3).

States Parties

(as of 1 March 1982)

Belgium
Luxembourg
Netherlands

2. The Nordic States Scheme and Nordic Treaty of 1962, *signed* Mar. 23, 1962, *entered into force* July 1, 1962, 434 U.N.T.S. 145.

Editor's Note

The Nordic Treaty, in which the Contracting States agree on broad principles of cooperation, is preceded by a specific agreement on extradition. Effect is given to the agreement by the enactment of similar legislation by each member State.

The Contracting Parties agree to grant extradition of persons suspected, accused or who have been convicted of an offense punishable by the law of the requesting State. Extradition by a State of its own nationals is not required unless the offense is one which by the law of the requested State carries a possible sentence of four years' penal servitude or more, or the fugitive has been domiciled in the requesting State for at least two years (Section 2).

In respect of political offenses, extradition is not permitted except when the offense is punishable by the law of the requested State and the person is not a national of that State (Section 4).

States Parties

(as of 1 March 1982)

Denmark
Finland
Iceland
Norway
Sweden

3. Arab League Extradition Agreement, *approved* Sept. 14, 1952, *entered into force* Aug. 28, 1954, *reprinted in* 159 B.F.S.P. 606 (1952) and 8 Revue Egyptienne de Droit International 328 (1952).

Editor's Note

The Agreement makes obligatory the extradition of persons pursued, charged with, or condemned for an offense punishable under the laws of both the requesting and requested States by imprisonment for one year or a heavier penalty (Articles 2 & 3). In the case of convicted offenders, the offense for which the fugitive was convicted must carry a sentence of two months' imprisonment or more (Article 3).

Extradition is not to be granted for political offenses subject to the qualification of a *Belgian* clause, *i.e.,* the assassination of Heads of States or their families, attempts against heirs to thrones, and premeditated murder or acts of terrorism are not to be regarded as political offenses (Article 4).

A State may refuse to extradite its own nationals, but if it exercises this right it must itself prosecute them for the same offense for which extradition was sought. The Agreement remains open for accession by any member State of the Arab League.

States Parties

(as of 1 March 1982)

Egypt
Jordan
Saudi Arabia

4. Scheme Relating to the Rendition of Fugitive Offenders Within the (British) Commonwealth (Commonwealth Scheme), H.M.S.O., London, Cmd. 3008 (1966).

Editor's Note

The Scheme envisages uniform legislation enacted in each member State of the Commonwealth.

The Scheme commits the member States to extradite offenders on an enumerated list of offenses (Annex 1), coupled with the requirement that they be punishable under the laws of the requesting State by imprisonment for 12 months or by a heavier penalty (Article 3).

The extradition of a State's own nationals is discretionary.

The extradition of fugitives for political offenses is prohibited. This prohibition includes requests for extradition which, although purporting to be made in respect of criminal offenses, in reality have been made for the purpose of prosecuting or punishing a fugitive on account of his race, religion, nationality, or political opinions (Article 9).

States Parties

(as of 1 March 1982)

Australia
Barbados
Botswana
Canada
Cyprus
Fiji
Gambia
Ghana
Guyana
India
Jamaica
Kenya
Lesotho
Malawi
Malaysia
Malta
Mauritius
New Zealand
Nigeria
Pakistan
Sierra Leone
Singapore
Sri Lanka
Swaziland
Tanzania
Trinidad and Tobago
Tonga
Uganda
United Kingdom

Western Samoa
Zambia

5. Bilateral Treaties of the Socialist States of Eastern Europe (*see, e.g.,* Treaty between Romania and Hungary of October 7, 1958, *signed* Oct. 7, 1958, *entered into force* May 7, 1959, 416 U.N.T.S. 199).

Editor's Note

Uniformity as regards extradition between individual members of the Soviet bloc has been achieved by a network of virtually identical bilateral treaties for legal assistance in civil, family and criminal cases.

In general, the Contracting Parties are required to extradite persons accused or convicted of offenses which, under the law of both the requested and requesting States, are punishable by imprisonment of one year or a heavier penalty. Extradition by a State of its own nationals is not required, but a State refusing to extradite is required to prosecute its nationals who are believed to have committed an extraditable offense in the territory of a State that requests extradition.

There are no provisions in the treaties prohibiting the extradition of political offenders.

States Parties

(as of 1 March 1982)

Bulgaria
Byelorussian S.S.R.
Czechoslovakia
German Democratic Republic

Hungary
Poland
Romania
Ukrainian S.S.R.
U.S.S.R.
Yugoslavia

6. Bilateral Treaty Relating to the Extradition of Hijackers
— Agreement on Hijacking of Aircraft and Vessels and
Other Offenses, Feb. 15, 1973, United States-Cuba, 24
U.S.T. 737, T.I.A.S. No. 7579 (*terminated* Apr. 15,
1977, 76 Dep't State Bull. 504 (1977)).

Editor's Note

Article 1 of the Agreement stipulates that a hijacker shall
be considered to have committed an offense and shall be
returned to the State of registry of the aircraft or vessel or
be brought before the courts of the party whose territory he
reached. If the offense is not punishable in that country, the
State is required to return the individual to the country of
registry of the aircraft or vessel. Each party also agrees to
take all necessary steps to facilitate the continuation of the
journey of the aircraft or vessel, its passengers, crew and
cargo.

The Agreement emphasizes severe punishment (Article
2) but grants an exception where the hijacker is being
sought for strictly political reasons and was in real and
imminent danger of death with no other alternative of
escape, provided there was no financial extortion or injury
to any person (Article 4).

157

U.S. Action

Hijacking Accord Between the United States and Cuba: Hearings Before the House Foreign Affairs Comm., 93d Cong., 1st Sess. (1973).

III. CONVENTIONS RELATING TO ASYLUM

A. General

1. Convention Relating to the Status of Refugees, *opened for signature* July 28, 1951, *entered into force* Apr. 22, 1954, 189 U.N.T.S. 137.

Editor's Note

The Convention contains the principle of *non-refoulement:*

> No Contracting State shall expel or return ("refouler") a refugee in any manner whatsoever to the frontiers of territories where his life or freedom would be threatened on account of his race, religion, nationality, membership of a particular social group or political opinion.

(Article 33). A refugee is defined as any person who:

> As a result of events occurring before 1 January 1951 and owing to well-founded fear of being persecuted for reasons of race, religion, nationality, membership of a particular social group, or political opinion, is outside the country of his nationality and is unable or, owing to such fear is unwilling to avail himself of the protection of that country; or who, not having a nationality and being outside the country of his former habitual residence as a result of such events, is unable or, owing to such fear, is unwilling to return to it.

158

(Article 1). However, the provisions of the Convention are not to apply to any person to whom there are serious reasons for considering that:

(a) he has committed a crime against peace, a war crime, or a crime against humanity, as defined in the international instruments drawn up to make provision in respect of such crimes;

(b) he has committed a serious non-political crime outside the country of refuge prior to his admission to that country as a refugee; [and]

(c) he has been guilty of acts contrary to the purposes and principles of the United Nations.

(Article 1).

States Parties

(as of 1 March 1982)

Algeria
Angola
Argentina
Australia
Austria
Belgium
Benin
Bolivia
Botswana
Brazil
Burundi
Cameroon
Canada
Central African Republic
Chad
Chile

Colombia
Congo
Costa Rica
Cyprus
Denmark
Djibouti
Dominican Republic
Ecuador
Egypt
Ethiopia
Fiji
Finland
France
Gabon
Gambia
Germany, Federal
    Republic of

159

Ghana	Panama
Greece	Paraguay
Guinea	Peru
Guinea-Bissau	Philippines
Holy See	Portugal
Iceland	Rwanda
Iran	Sao Tome and Principe
Ireland	Senegal
Israel	Seychelles
Italy	Sierra Leone
Ivory Coast	Somalia
Jamaica	Spain
Japan	Sudan
Kenya	Sweden
Lesotho	Switzerland
Liberia	Tanzania
Liechtenstein	Togo
Luxembourg	Tunisia
Madagascar	Turkey
Mali	Uganda
Malta	United Kingdom
Monaco	Upper Volta
Morocco	Uruguay
Netherlands	Yemen, Democratic
New Zealand	Yugoslavia
Nicaragua	Zaire
Niger	Zambia
Nigeria	Zimbabwe
Norway	

Cases

FEDERAL

District Court

Fernandez-Roque v. Smith, 91 F.R.D. 117, 120 (N.D. Ga. 1981).

2. Protocol Relating to the Status of Refugees, *signed* Jan. 21, 1967, *entered into force* Oct. 4, 1967, 19 U.S.T. 6223, T.I.A.S. No. 6577, 606 U.N.T.S. 267 (*entered into force* for U.S. Nov. 1, 1968).

Editor's Note

The Protocol, which extends the scope of the *Convention Relating to the Status of Refugees* by including persons becoming refugees as a result of events occurring since 1 January 1951, incorporates the substantive provisions of the Convention, including Article 33 embodying the principle of *non-refoulement.*

States Parties

(as of 1 March 1982)

Algeria	Bolivia
Argentina	Botswana
Australia	Brazil
Austria	Burundi
Belgium	Cameroon
Benin	Canada

Central African Republic
Chad
Chile
Colombia
Congo
Costa Rica
Cyprus
Denmark
Djibouti
Dominican Republic
Ecuador
Egypt
Ethiopia
Fiji
Finland
France
Gabon
Gambia
Germany, Federal Republic
  of
Ghana
Greece
Guinea
Guinea-Bissau
Holy See
Iceland
Iran
Ireland
Israel
Italy
Ivory Coast
Jamaica
Japan

Kenya
Lesotho
Liberia
Liechtenstein
Luxembourg
Mali
Malta
Morocco
Netherlands
New Zealand
Nicaragua
Niger
Nigeria
Norway
Panama
Paraguay
Philippines
Portugal
Rwanda
Sao Tome and Principe
Senegal
Seychelles
Sierra Leone
Somalia
Spain
Sudan
Surinam
Swaziland
Sweden
Switzerland
Tanzania
Togo
Tunisia

Turkey
Uganda
United Kingdom
United States
Upper Volta
Uruguay

Yemen, Democratic
Yugoslavia
Zaire
Zambia
Zimbabwe

U.S. Action

Message from the President Transmitting the Protocol Relating to the Status of Refugees, S. Exec. Doc. K, 90th Cong., 2d Sess. (1968).

Protocol Relating to the Status of Refugees: Hearings Before the Senate Comm. on Foreign Relations, 90th Cong., 2d Sess. (1968).

Senate Comm. on Foreign Relations, Report on the Protocol Relating to the Status of Refugees, S. Exec. Rep. 14, 90th Cong., 2d Sess. (1968).

Cases

FEDERAL

Supreme Court

Immigration & Naturalization Serv. v. Stanisic, 395 U.S. 65, 79 n.22 (1969).

Court of Appeals

Sindona v. Grant, 619 F.2d 167, 174 (2d Cir. 1980), aff'g In re Sindona, 450 F. Supp. 672, 694 (S.D.N.Y. 1978); Sindona v. Grant, 461 F. Supp. 199 (S.D.N.Y. 1978).

Huynh Thi Anh v. Levi, 586 F.2d 625, 629 (6th Cir. 1978).

Coriolan v. Immigration & Naturalization Serv., 559 F.2d 993, 996-97 (5th Cir. 1977).

Kashani v. Immigration & Naturalization Serv., 547 F.2d 376, 379-90 (7th Cir. 1977).

Cisternas-Estay v. Immigration & Naturalization Serv., 531 F.2d 155, 158, 160 (3d Cir.), *cert. denied,* 429 U.S. 853 (1976).

Pierre v. United States, 525 F.2d 933, 935 (5th Cir. 1976); 547 F.2d 1281, 1284-89 (5th Cir. 1977), *vacated and remanded,* 434 U.S. 962 (1978).

Cheng v. Immigration & Naturalization Serv., 521 F.2d 1351, 1352 n.5 (3d Cir. 1975), *cert. denied,* 423 U.S. 1051 (1976).

Paul v. United States Immigration & Naturalization Serv., 521 F.2d 194, 205 (5th Cir. 1975) (Godbold, J., dissenting).

Yu Fung Cheng v. Rinaldi, 493 F.2d 1229, 1229 (3d Cir.), *cert. denied,* 419 U.S. 874 (1974).

Nicosia v. Wall, 442 F.2d 1005, 1006 (5th Cir. 1971).

Muskardin v. Immigration & Naturalization Serv., 415 F.2d 865, 867 (2d Cir. 1969).

District Court

Vigile v. Sava, 535 F. Supp. 1002, 1018-20 (S.D.N.Y. 1982).

Haitian Refugee Center v. Civiletti, 503 F. Supp. 442, 453 n.16, 482 (S.D. Fla. 1980).

Ahmad v. Morris, 461 F. Supp. 123, 126, 127 (E.D. Pa. 1978).

Sannon v. United States, 427 F. Supp. 1270, 1274, 1276-77 (S.D. Fla. 1977), *vacated mem.,* 566 F.2d 104 (5th Cir. 1978); 460 F. Supp. 458, 459-60 (S.D. Fla. 1978).

Yan Wo Cheng v. Rinaldi, 389 F. Supp. 583, 585 (D.N.J. 1975).

Chim Ming v. Marks, 367 F. Supp. 673, 676-81 (S.D.N.Y. 1973), *aff'd,* 505 F.2d 1170, 1171-72 (2d Cir. 1974), *cert. denied,* 421 U.S. 911 (1975).

Kan Kim Lin v. Rinaldi, 361 F. Supp. 177, 179 n.1, 183-86 (D.N.J. 1973), aff'd, 493 F.2d 1229 (3d Cir.), cert. denied, 419 U.S. 874 (1974).

B. African Convention on Asylum

1. Convention of the Organization of African Unity (O.A.U.) Governing the Specific Aspects of Refugee Problems in Africa, adopted Sept. 10, 1969, entered into force Nov. 26, 1973, reprinted in 8 Int'l Legal Materials 1288 (1969).

Editor's Note

The Convention is the regional complement of the 1951 Convention Relating to the Status of Refugees and the 1967 Protocol.

The definition of the term refugee as contained in the O.A.U. Convention is closely modelled on the definition of the 1951 Convention and 1967 Protocol with their concept of well-founded fear of persecution, except that it also includes individuals generally seeking refuge from violence of any kind of foreign occupation whether or not in fear of persecution (Article 1).

The exclusion clauses of the definition likewise are similar, except that they contain an additional ground, i.e., excluded also are persons with respect to whom the country of asylum has serious reasons for considering that they have been guilty of acts contrary to the purposes and principles of the O.A.U. These relevant purposes and principles are:

> unreserved condemnation, in all its forms, of political assassination as well as subversive activities on the part of neighboring States or any other State;

165

absolute dedication to the total emancipation of the African territories which are still dependent.

(Charter of the Organization of African Unity [Addis Ababa 1968]).

The O.A.U. Convention regulates the question of asylum. Article 2 contains the principle of a grant of asylum, although its wording is recommendatory rather than mandatory: "Member States of the O.A.U. shall use their best endeavors consistent with their respective legislations to receive refugees . . . ." Further, Article 2 expands the principle of *non-refoulement* to include rejection at the frontier:

> No person shall be subjected . . . to measures such as rejection, return or expulsion, which would compel him to return or to remain in a territory where his life, physical integrity or liberty would be threatened. . . .

The O.A.U. Convention contains important provisions on subversion, which prohibit a refugee from engaging in any subversive activities against any Member State of the O.A.U. and impose a positive duty on the Contracting States to prohibit such activities (Article 3).

States Parties

(as of 1 March 1982)

Algeria
Benin
Central African Republic
Congo
Dahomey
Ethiopia
Guinea
Liberia

Mauritania
Niger
Senegal
Sudan
Togo
Zaire
Zambia

C. Inter-American Conventions on Asylum

1. 1928 Convention on Asylum, *signed* Feb. 20, 1928, 132
   L.N.T.S. 323.

Editor's Note

The Convention delimits the rules for granting of asylum.
The Convention prohibits States "to grant asylum in
legations, warships, military camps or military aircraft, to
persons accused or condemned for common crimes ...."
(Article 1). Individuals accused of or condemned for common
crimes found in any of the above places are to be
surrendered upon request (Article 1). However, asylum
granted in such places to political offenders shall be
respected subject to the condition of urgency (*i.e.*, that
asylum be granted only in urgent cases) (Article 2). The
Convention is still in force.

States Parties

(as of 1 March 1982)

Brazil
Colombia

Costa Rica
Cuba
Ecuador
El Salvador
Guatemala
Haiti
Honduras
Mexico
Nicaragua
Panama
Paraguay
Peru
Uruguay

2. 1933 Convention on Political Asylum, *signed* Dec. 26, 1933, *entered into force* Mar. 28, 1935, 6 *Hudson* 607 (1937).

Editor's Note

The Convention, amending the 1928 Convention in part, provides that asylum shall not be granted "to those accused of common offenses who may have been duly prosecuted or who may have been sentenced by ordinary courts of justice...." (Article 1).

The Convention confers upon the State offering asylum the right to decide whether an offense is political or not (Article 2). Further, the Convention stipulates that political asylum, as an institution of humanitarian character, is not subject to reciprocity. The Convention is still in force.

States Parties

(as of 1 March 1982)

Argentina
Brazil
Chile
Colombia
Costa Rica
Cuba
Ecuador
El Salvador
Guatemala
Haiti
Honduras
Mexico
Nicaragua
Panama
Paraguay
Peru

3. 1939 Treaty on Asylum and Political Refuge, *signed* Aug. 4, 1939, 8 Hudson 404 (1949).

Editor's Note

This Treaty, which is more elaborate than the 1933 Convention on Political Asylum in laying down rules on the granting of asylum, stipulates that political asylum will be granted exclusively to individuals pursued for political reasons or to individuals having committed offenses which do not legally permit extradition (Article 2). However, diplomatic asylum shall not be granted to persons accused of political offenses who have been indicted or condemned previously for common offenses (Article 3).

Persons benefiting from asylum granted pursuant to the Treaty cannot participate in or attempt to influence political activities (Article 5). Moreover, the State granting asylum may impose rigid restrictions on them (Articles 5 & 6). While the Treaty has no provision regarding the number of ratifications necessary for it to come into effect, Article 18 provides that it "shall go into effect among the high contracting parties in the order in which they have deposited their ratifications." It appears, therefore, to be binding on States which have signed it.

States Parties

(as of 1 March 1982)

Paraguay
Peru
Uruguay

4. 1954 Convention on Territorial Asylum, *signed* Mar. 28, 1954, Pan-Am T.S. No. 19, *reprinted in* 161 B.F.S.P. 566.

Editor's Note

The Convention confirms the sovereign right of the State to admit into its territory such individuals as it deems advisable (Articles 1 & 2). Article 3 stipulates that no State is under an obligation to surrender to another State persons persecuted for political reasons or offenses. Further, States are not required to extradite persons who, in the opinion of the requested State, are sought for political offenses, or for common offenses committed for political ends. Surreptitious or irregular entry does not affect the provisions of the Convention.

The Convention requires asylum-granting States, upon the request of another State, to take steps to keep watch over, or to intern at a reasonable distance from its border, those political refugees who are notorious leaders of subversive movements as well as those refugees against whom there is evidence of a disposition to join such a movement (Article 9). The Convention is still in force.

States Parties

(as of 1 March 1982)

Brazil
Colombia
Costa Rica
Ecuador
El Salvador
Haiti
Mexico
Panama
Paraguay
Uruguay
Venezuela

5. 1954 Convention on Diplomatic Asylum, *signed* Mar. 28, 1954, Pan-Am T.S. No. 18, *reprinted in* 161 B.F.S.P. 570.

Editor's Note

The Convention provides that asylum granted in legations, warships, and military camps or aircraft to persons being sought for political reasons or offenses is to be respected by the territorial State (Articles 1 & 2), subject to the conditions of urgency and limitation of time (Article 5). While a State has the right to grant asylum, it is not obligated to do so or to give reasons for refusing asylum.

This right of a State is not without limitations. Asylum is not to be granted to persons who at the time of requesting it are under indictment or on trial or have been convicted for common offenses, save when the acts giving rise to the request are clearly of a political nature (Article 3). The State granting asylum is given the right to determine the nature of the offense or the motives for prosecution (Article 4).

Further, asylum is to be granted only in urgent cases and should not be extended beyond the period of time strictly necessary in order to get a guarantee from the Government of the territorial State to the effect that the refugee may depart from the country without his life, liberty or political integrity being endangered, or in order to ensure the safety of the refugee in some other way (Article 5). Urgent cases are ones in which the individual for political reasons is being sought by the authorities, or by persons or mobs over whom the authorities have lost control, and is in danger of being deprived of his life or liberty and cannot, without risk, ensure his safety in any other way. The State granting asylum has the right to determine the degree or urgency in each case (Article 7). The Convention is still in force.

States Parties

(as of 1 March 1982)

Brazil
Costa Rica
Dominican Republic
Ecuador

El Salvador
Mexico
Panama
Paraguay
Peru
Uruguay
Venezuela

Appendix I

PAST EFFORTS

1. League of Nations 1937 Convention for the Prevention and Punishment of Terrorism, *opened for signature* Nov. 16, 1937, League of Nations Doc. C.546(I). M.383(I) (1937).

ARTICLE 1

1. The High Contracting Parties, reaffirming the principle of international law in virtue of which it is the duty of every State to refrain from any act designed to encourage terrorist activities directed against another State and to prevent the acts in which such activities take shape, undertake as hereinafter provided to prevent and punish activities of this nature and to collaborate for this purpose.

2. In the present Convention, the expression "acts of terrorism" means criminal acts directed against a State and intended or calculated to create a state of terror in the minds of particular persons, or a group of persons or the general public.

ARTICLE 2

Each of the High Contracting Parties shall, if this has not already been done, make the following acts committed on his own territory criminal offences if they are directed against another High Contracting Party and if they constitute acts of terrorism within the meaning of Article 1:

(1) Any wilful act causing death or grievous bodily harm or loss of liberty to:

(a) Heads of States, persons exercising the prerogatives of the head of the State, their hereditary or designated successors;

175

(b) The wives or husbands of the above-mentioned persons;

(c) Persons charged with public functions or holding public positions when the act is directed against them in their public capacity.

(2) Wilful destruction of, or damage to, public property or property devoted to a public purpose belonging to or subject to the authority of another High Contracting Party.

(3) Any wilful act calculated to endanger the lives of members of the public.

(4) Any attempt to commit an offence falling within the foregoing provisions of the present article.

(5) The manufacture, obtaining, possession, or supplying of arms, ammunition, explosives or harmful substances with a view to the commission in any country whatsoever of an offence falling within the present article.

ARTICLE 3

Each of the High Contracting Parties shall make the following acts criminal offences when they are committed on his own territory with a view to an act of terrorism falling within Article 2 and directed against another High Contracting Party, whatever the country in which the act of terrorism is to be carried out:

(1) Conspiracy to commit any such act;

(2) Any incitement to any such act, if successful;

(3) Direct public incitement to any act mentioned under heads (1), (2) or (3) of Article 2, whether the incitement be successful or not;

(4) Wilful participation in any such act;

(5) Assistance, knowingly given, towards the commission of any such act.

ARTICLE 4

Each of the offences mentioned in Article 3 shall be treated by the law as a distinct offence in all cases where this is necessary in order to prevent an offender escaping punishment.

ARTICLE 5

Subject to any special provisions of national law for the protection of the persons mentioned under head (1) of Article 2, or of the property mentioned under head (2) of Article 2, each High Contracting Party shall provide the same punishment for the acts set out in Articles 2 and 3, whether they be directed against that or another High Contracting Party.

ARTICLE 6

1. In countries where the principle of the international recognition of previous convictions is accepted, foreign convictions for any of the offences mentioned in Articles 2 and 3 will, within the conditions prescribed by domestic law, be taken into account for the purpose of establishing habitual criminality.

2. Such convictions will, further, in the case of High Contracting Parties whose law recognises foreign convictions, be taken into account, with or without special proceedings, for the purpose of imposing, in the manner provided by that law, incapacities, disqualifications or interdictions whether in the sphere of public or of private law.

ARTICLE 7

In so far as *parties civiles* are admitted under the domestic law, foreign *parties civiles,* including, in proper cases, a High Contracting Party shall be entitled to all rights allowed to nationals by the law of the country in which the case is tried.

ARTICLE 8

1. Without prejudice to the provisions of paragraph 4 below, the offences set out in Articles 2 and 3 shall be deemed to be included as extradition crimes in any extradition treaty which has been, or may hereafter be, concluded between any of the High Contracting Parties.

2. The High Contracting Parties who do not make extradition conditional on the existence of a treaty shall henceforward, without prejudice to the provisions of paragraph 4 below and subject to reciprocity, recognise the offences set out in Articles 2 and 3 as extradition crimes as between themselves.

3. For the purposes of the present article, any offence specified in Articles 2 and 3, if committed in the territory of the High Contracting Party against whom it is directed, shall also be deemed to be an extradition crime.

4. The obligation to grant extradition under the present article shall be subject to any conditions and limitations recognised by the law or the practice of the country to which application is made.

ARTICLE 9

1. When the principle of the extradition of nationals is not recognised by a High Contracting Party, nationals who have returned to the territory of their own country after the

commission abroad of an offence mentioned in Articles 2 or 3 shall be prosecuted and punished in the same manner as if the offence had been committed on that territory, even in a case where the offender has acquired his nationality after the commission of the offence.

2. The provisions of the present article shall not apply if, in similar circumstances, the extradition of a foreigner cannot be granted.

ARTICLE 10

Foreigners who are on the territory of a High Contracting Party and who have committed abroad any of the offences set out in Articles 2 and 3 shall be prosecuted and punished as though the offence had been committed in the territory of that High Contracting Party, if the following conditions are fulfilled — namely, that:

(a) Extradition has been demanded and could not be granted for a reason not connected with the offence itself;

(b) The law of the country of refuge recognises the jurisdiction of its own courts in respect of offences committed abroad by foreigners;

(c) The foreigner is a national of a country which recognises the jurisdiction of its own courts in respect of offences committed abroad by foreigners.

ARTICLE 11

1. The provisions of Articles 9 and 10 shall also apply to offences referred to in Articles 2 and 3 which have been committed in the territory of the High Contracting Party against whom they were directed.

2. As regards the application of Articles 9 and 10, the High Contracting Parties do not undertake to pass a sen-

tence exceeding the maximum sentence provided by the law of the country where the offence was committed.

ARTICLE 12

Each High Contracting Party shall take on his own territory and within the limits of his own law and administrative organisation the measures which he considers appropriate for the effective prevention of all activities contrary to the purpose of the present Convention.

ARTICLE 13

1. Without prejudice to the provisions of head (5) of Article 2, the carrying, possession and distribution of fire-arms, other than smooth-bore sporting-guns, and of ammunition shall be subjected to regulation. It shall be a punishable offence to transfer, sell or distribute such arms or munitions to any person who does not hold such licence or make such declaration as may be required by domestic legislation concerning the possession and carrying of such articles; this shall apply also to the transfer, sale or distribution of explosives.

2. Manufacturers of fire-arms, other than smooth-bore sporting-guns, shall be required to mark each arm with a serial number or other distinctive mark permitting it to be identified; both manufacturers and retailers shall be obliged to keep a register of the names and addresses of purchasers.

ARTICLE 14

1. The following acts shall be punishable:

(a) Any fraudulent manufacture or alteration of passports or other equivalent documents;

(b) Bringing into the country, obtaining or being in possession of such forged or falsified documents knowing them to be forged or falsified;

(c) Obtaining such documents by means of false declarations or documents;

(d) Wilfully using any such documents which are forged or falsified or were made out for a person other than the bearer.

2. The wilful issue of passports, other equivalent documents, or visas by competent officials to persons known not to have the right thereto under the laws or regulations applicable, with the object of assisting any activity contrary to the purpose of the present Convention, shall also be punishable.

3. The provisions of the present article shall apply irrespective of the national or foreign character of the document.

Article 15

1. Results of the investigation of offences mentioned in Articles 2 and 3 and (where there may be a connection between the offence and preparations for an act of terrorism) in Article 14 shall in each country, subject to the provisions of its law, be centralised in an appropriate service.

2. Such service shall be in close contact:

(a) With the police authorities of the country;

(b) With the corresponding services in other countries.

3. It shall furthermore bring together all information calculated to facilitate the prevention and punishment of the offences mentioned in Articles 2 and 3 and (where there may be a connection between the offence and preparations

for an act of terrorism) in Article 14; it shall, as far as possible, keep in close contact with the judicial authorities of the country.

ARTICLE 16

Each service, so far as it considers it desirable to do so, shall notify to the services of the other countries, giving all necessary particulars:

(a) Any act mentioned in Articles 2 and 3, even if it has not been carried into effect, such notification to be accompanied by descriptions, copies and photographs;

(b) Any search for, any prosecution, arrest, conviction or expulsion of persons guilty of offences dealt with in the present Convention, the movements of such persons and any pertinent information with regard to them, as well as their description, finger-prints and photographs;

(c) Discovery of documents, arms, appliances or other objects connected with offences mentioned in Articles 2, 3, 13 and 14.

ARTICLE 17

1. The High Contracting Parties shall be bound to execute letters of request relating to offences referred to in the present Convention in accordance with their domestic law and practice and any international convictions concluded or to be concluded by them.

2. The transmission of letters of request shall be effected:

(a) By direct communication between the judicial authorities;

(b) By direct correspondence between the Ministers of Justice of the two countries;

182

(c) By direct correspondence between the authority of the country making the request and the Minister of Justice of the country to which the request is made;

(d) Through the diplomatic or consular representative of the country making the request in the country to which the request is made; this representative shall send the letters of request, either directly or through the Minister for Foreign Affairs, to the competent judicial authority or to the authority indicated by the Governor of the country to which the request is made and shall receive the papers constituting the execution of the letters of request from this authority either directly or through the Minister for Foreign Affairs.

3. In cases (a) and (d), a copy of the letters of request shall always be sent simultaneously to the Minister of Justice of the country to which application is made.

4. Unless otherwise agreed, the letters of request shall be drawn up in the language of the authority making the request, provided always that the country to which the request is made may require a translation in its own language, certified correct by the authority making the request.

5. Each High Contracting Party shall notify to each of the other High Contracting Parties the method or methods of transmission mentioned above which he will recognise for the letters of request of the latter High Contracting Party.

6. Until such notification is made by a High Contracting Party, his existing procedure in regard to letters of request shall remain in force.

7. Execution of letters of request shall not give rise to a claim for reimbursement of charges or expenses of any nature whatever other than expenses of experts.

8. Nothing in the present article shall be construed as an undertaking on the part of the High Contracting Parties to adopt in criminal matters any form or methods of proof contrary to their laws.

ARTICLE 18

The participation of a High Contracting Party in the present Convention shall not be interpreted as affecting that Party's attitude on the general question of the limits of criminal jurisdiction as a question of international law.

ARTICLE 19

The present Convention does not affect the principle that, provided the offender is not allowed to escape punishment owing to an omission in the criminal law, the characterisation of the various offences dealt with in the present Convention, the imposition of sentences, the methods of prosecution and trial, and the rules as to mitigating circumstances; pardon and amnesty are determined in each country by the provisions of domestic law.

ARTICLE 20

1. If any dispute should arise between the High Contracting Parties relating to the interpretation or application of the present Convention, and if such dispute has not been satisfactorily solved by diplomatic means, it shall be settled in conformity with the provisions in force between the parties concerning the settlement of international disputes.

2. If such provisions should not exist between the parties to the dispute, the parties shall refer the dispute to an arbitral or judicial procedure. If no agreement is reached on

the choice of another court, the parties shall refer the dispute to the Permanent Court of International Justice, if they are all parties to the Protocol of December 16th, 1920, relating to the Statute of that Court; and if they are not all parties to that Protocol, they shall refer the dispute to a court of arbitration constituted in accordance with the Convention of The Hague of October 18th, 1907, for the Pacific Settlement of International Disputes.

3. The above provisions of the present article shall not prevent High Contracting Parties, if they are Members of the League of Nations, from bringing the dispute before the Council or the Assembly of the League if the Covenant gives them the power to do so.

ARTICLE 21

1. The present Convention, of which the French and English texts shall be both authentic, shall bear to-day's date. Until May 31st, 1938, it shall be open for signature on behalf of any Member of the League of Nations and on behalf of any non-member State represented at the Conference which drew up the present Convention or to which a copy thereof is communicated for this purpose by the Council of the League of Nations.

2. The present Convention shall be ratified. The instruments of ratification shall be transmitted to the Secretary-General of the League of Nations to be deposited in the archives of the League; the Secretary-General shall notify their deposit to all the members of the League and to the non-member States mentioned in the preceding paragraph.

ARTICLE 22

1. After June 1st, 1938, the present Convention shall be open to accession by any Member of the League of Nations, and any of the non-member States referred to in Article 21, on whose behalf the Convention has not been signed.

2. The instruments of accession shall be transmitted to the Secretary-General of the League of Nations to be deposited in the archives of the League; the Secretary-General shall notify their receipt to all the Members of the League and to the non-member States referred to in Article 21.

ARTICLE 23

1. Any Member of the League of Nations or non-member State which is prepared to ratify the Convention under the second paragraph of Article 21, or to accede to the Convention under Article 22, but desires to be allowed to make reservations with regard to the application of the Convention, may so inform the Secretary-General of the League of Nations, who shall forthwith communicate such reservations to all the Members of the League and non-member States on whose behalf ratifications or accessions have been deposited and enquire whether they have any objection thereto. Should the reservation be formulated within three years from the entry into force of the Convention, the same enquiry shall be addressed to Members of the League and non-member States whose signature of the Convention has not yet been followed by ratification. If, within six months from the date of the Secretary-General's communication, no objection to the reservation has been made, it shall be treated as accepted by the High Contracting Parties.

2. In the event of any objection being received, the Secretary-General of the League of Nations shall inform the Government which desired to make the reservation and request it to inform him whether it is prepared to ratify or accede without the reservation or whether it prefers to abstain from ratification or accession.

ARTICLE 24

Ratification of, or accession to, the present Convention by any High Contracting Party implies an assurance by him that his legislation and his administrative organisation enable him to give effect to the provisions of the present Convention.

ARTICLE 25

1. Any High Contracting Party may declare, at the time of signature, ratification or accession, that, in accepting the present Convention, he is not assuming any obligation in respect of all or any of his colonies, protectorates, oversea territories, territories under his suzerainty or territories in respect of which a mandate has been entrusted to him; the present Convention shall, in that case, not be applicable to the territories named in such declaration.

2. Any High Contracting Party may subsequently notify the Secretary-General of the League of Nations that he desires the present Convention to apply to all or any of the territories in respect of which the declaration provided for in the preceding paragraph has been made. In making such notification, the High Contracting Party concerned may state that the application of the Convention to any of such territories shall be subject to any reservations which have been accepted in respect of that High Contracting Party under Article 23. The Convention shall then apply, with

any such reservations, to all the territories named in such notification ninety days after the receipt thereof by the Secretary-General of the League of Nations. Should it be desired as regards any such territories to make reservations other than those already made under Article 23 by the High Contracting Party concerned, the procedure set out in that Article shall be followed.

3. Any High Contracting Party may at any time declare that he desires the present Convention to cease to apply to all or any of his colonies, protectorates, oversea territories, territories under his suzerainty or territories in respect of which a mandate has been entrusted to him. The Convention shall, in that case, cease to apply to the territories named in such declaration one year after the receipt of this declaration by the Secretary-General of the League of Nations.

4. The Secretary-General of the League of Nations shall communicate to all the Members of the League of Nations and to the non-member States referred to in Article 21 the declarations and notifications received in virtue of the present Article.

ARTICLE 26

1. The present Convention shall, in accordance with the provisions of Article 18 of the Covenant, be registered by the Secretary-General of the League of Nations on the ninetieth day after the receipt by the Secretary-General of the third instrument of ratification or accession.

2. The Convention shall come into force on the date of such registration.

ARTICLE 27

Each ratification or accession taking place after the deposit of the third instrument of ratification or accession shall take effect on the ninetieth day following the date on which the instrument of ratification or accession is received by the Secretary-General of the League of Nations.

ARTICLE 28

A request for the revision of the present Convention may be made at any time by any High Contracting Party by means of a notification to the Secretary-General of the League of Nations. Such notification shall be communicated by the Secretary-General to all the other High Contracting Parties and, if it is supported by at least a third of those Parties, the High Contracting Parties undertake to hold a conference for the revision of the Convention.

ARTICLE 29

The present Convention may be denounced on behalf of any High Contracting Party by a notification in writing addressed to the Secretary-General of the League of Nations, who shall inform all the Members of the League and the non-member States referred to in Article 21. Such a denunciation shall take effect one year after the date of its receipt by the Secretary-General of the League of Nations, and shall be operative only in respect of the High Contracting Party on whose behalf it was made.

In Faith Whereof the Plenipotentiaries have signed the present Convention.

Done at Geneva, on the sixteenth day of November one thousand nine hundred and thirty-seven, in a single copy, which will be deposited in the archives of the Secretariat of the League of Nations; a certified true copy thereof shall be transmitted to all the Members of the League of Nations and all the non-member States referred to in Article 21.

2. 1972 United States Draft Convention for the Prevention and Punishment of Certain Acts of International Terrorism, *reprinted in* 67 Dep't State Bull. 431 (1972).

The States Parties to This Convention —
Recalling United Nations General Assembly Resolution 2625 (XXV) proclaiming principles of international law concerning friendly relations and co-operation among States in accordance with the Charter of the United Nations;

Considering that this Resolution provides that every State has the duty to refrain from organizing, instigating, assisting or participating in terrorist acts in another State or acquiescing in organized activities within its territory directed towards the commission of such acts;

Considering the common danger posed by the spread of terrorist acts across national boundaries;

Considering that civilians must be protected from terrorist acts;

Affirming that effective measures to control international terrorism are urgently needed and require international as well as national action;

Have agreed as follows:

ARTICLE 1

1. Any person who unlawfully kills, causes serious bodily harm or kidnaps another person, attempts to commit any such act, or participates as an accomplice of a person who

190

commits or attempts to commit any such act, commits an offense of international significance if the act:

(a) is committed or takes effect outside the territory of a State of which the alleged offender is a national; and

(b) is committed or takes effect:

(i) outside the territory of the State against which the act is directed, or

(ii) within the territory of the State against which the act is directed and the alleged offender knows or has reason to know that a person against whom the act is directed is not a national of that State; and

(c) is committed neither by nor against a member of the Armed Forces of a State in the course of military hostilities; and

(d) is intended to damage the interests of or obtain concessions from a State or an international organization.

2. For the purposes of this Convention:

(a) An "international organization" means an international intergovernmental organization.

(b) An "alleged offender" means a person as to whom there are grounds to believe that he has committed one or more of the offenses of international significance set forth in this Article.

(c) The "territory" of a State includes all territory under the jurisdiction or administration of the State.

ARTICLE 2

Each State Party undertakes to make the offenses set forth in Article 1 punishable by severe penalties.

ARTICLE 3

A State Party in whose territory an alleged offender is found shall, if it does not extradite him, submit, without exception whatsoever and without undue delay, the case to its competent authorities for the purpose of prosecution, through proceedings in accordance with the laws of that State.

ARTICLE 4

1. Each State Party shall take such measures as may be necessary to establish its jurisdiction over the offenses set forth in Article 1:

    (a) when the offense is committed in its territory, or

    (b) when the offense is committed by its national.

2. Each State Party shall likewise take such measures as may be necessary to establish its jurisdiction over the offenses set forth in Article 1 in the case where an alleged offender is present in its territory and the State does not extradite him to any of the States mentioned in Paragraph 1 of this Article.

3. This Convention does not exclude any criminal jurisdiction exercised in accordance with national law.

ARTICLE 5

A State Party in which one or more of the offenses set forth in Article 1 have been committed shall, if it has reason to believe an alleged offender has fled from its territory, communicate to all other States Parties all the pertinent facts regarding the offense committed and all available information regarding the identity of the alleged offender.

ARTICLE 6

1. The State Party in whose territory an alleged offender is found shall take appropriate measures under its internal law so as to ensure his presence for prosecution or extradition. Such measures shall be immediately notified to the States mentioned in Article 4, Paragraph 1, and all other interested States.

2. Any person regarding whom the measures referred to in Paragraph 1 of this Article are being taken shall be entitled to communicate immediately with the nearest appropriate representative of the State of which he is a national and to be visited by a representative of that State.

ARTICLE 7

1. To the extent that the offenses set forth in Article 1 are not listed as extraditable offenses in any extradition treaty existing between States Parties they shall be deemed to have been included as such therein. States Parties undertake to include those offenses as extraditable offenses in every future extradition treaty to be concluded between them.

2. If a State Party which makes extradition conditional on the existence of a treaty receives a request for extradition from another State Party with which it has no extradition treaty, it may, if it decides to extradite, consider the present articles as the legal basis for extradition in respect of the offenses. Extradition shall be subject to the provisions of the law of the requested State.

3. States Parties which do not make extradition conditional upon the existence of a treaty shall recognize the offenses as extraditable offenses between themselves subject to the provisions of the law of the requested State.

4. Each of the offenses shall be treated, for the purpose of extradition between States Parties as if it has been committed not only in the place in which it occurred but also in the territories of the States required to establish their jurisdiction in accordance with Article 4, Paragraph 1(b).

5. An extradition request from the State in which the offenses were committed shall have priority over other such requests if received by the State Party in whose territory the alleged offender has been found within thirty days after the communication required in Paragraph 1 of Article 6 has been made.

ARTICLE 8

Any person regarding whom proceedings are being carried out in connection with any of the offenses set forth in Article 1 shall be guaranteed fair treatment at all stages of the proceedings.

ARTICLE 9

The statutory limitation as to the time within which prosecution may be instituted for the offenses set forth in Article 1 shall be, in each State Party, that fixed for the most serious crimes under its internal law.

ARTICLE 10

1. States Parties shall, in accordance with international and national law, endeavor to take all practicable measures for the purpose of preventing the offenses set forth in Article 1.

2. Any State Party having reason to believe that one of the offenses set forth in Article 1 may be committed shall, in accordance with its national law, furnish any relevant

information in its possession to those States which it believes would be the States mentioned in Article 4, Paragraph 1, if any such offense were committed.

ARTICLE 11

1. States Parties shall afford one another the greatest measure of assistance in connection with criminal proceedings brought in respect of the offenses set forth in Article 1, including the supply of all evidence at their disposal necessary for the proceedings.

2. The provisions of Paragraph 1 of this Article shall not affect obligations concerning mutual assistance embodied in any other treaty.

ARTICLE 12

States Parties shall consult together for the purpose of considering and implementing such other cooperative measures as may seem useful for carrying out the purposes of this Convention.

ARTICLE 13

In any case in which one or more of the Geneva Conventions of August 12, 1949, or any other convention concerning the law of armed conflicts is applicable, such conventions shall, if in conflict with any provision of this Convention, take precedence. In particular:

(a) nothing in this Convention shall make an offense of any act which is permissible under the Geneva Convention Relative to the Protection of Civilian Persons in Time of War or any other international law applicable in armed conflicts; and

(b) nothing in this Convention shall deprive any person of prisoner of war status if entitled to such status under the Geneva Convention Relative to the Treatment of Prisoners of War or any other applicable convention concerning respect for human rights in armed conflicts.

ARTICLE 14

In any case in which the Convention on Offenses and Certain Other Acts Committed on Board Aircraft, the Convention for the Suppression of Unlawful Seizure of Aircraft, the Convention for the Suppression of Unlawful Acts Against the Safety of Civil Aviation, the Convention to Prevent and Punish the Acts of Terrorism Taking the Form of Crimes Against Persons and Related Extortion that Are of International Significance, or any other convention which has or may be concluded concerning the protection of civil aviation, diplomatic agents and other internationally protected persons, is applicable, such convention shall, if in conflict with any provision of this Convention, take precedence.

ARTICLE 15

Nothing in this Convention shall derogate from any obligations of the Parties under the United Nations Charter.

ARTICLE 16

1. Any dispute between the Parties arising out of the application or interpretation of the present articles that is not settled through negotiation may be brought by any State party to the dispute before a Conciliation Commission to be constituted in accordance with the provisions of this Article by the giving of written notice to the other State or

States Party to the dispute and to the Secretary-General of the United Nations.

2. A Conciliation Commission will be composed of three members. One member shall be appointed by each party to the dispute. If there is more than one party on either side of the dispute they shall jointly appoint a member of the Conciliation Commission. These two appointments shall be made within two months of the written notice referred to in Paragraph 1. The third member, the Chairman, shall be chosen by the other two members.

3. If either side has failed to appoint its members within the time limit referred to in Paragraph 2, the Secretary-General of the United Nations shall appoint such member within a further period of two months. If no agreement is reached on the choice of the Chairman within five months of the written notice referred to in Paragraph 1, the Secretary-General shall within the further period of one month appoint as the Chairman a qualified jurist who is not a national of any State party to the dispute.

4. Any vacancy shall be filled in the same manner as the original appointment was made.

5. The Commission shall establish its own rules of procedure and shall reach its decisions and recommendations by a majority vote. It shall be competent to ask any organ that is authorized by or in accordance with the Charter of the United Nations to request an advisory opinion from the International Court of Justice to make such a request regarding the interpretation or application of the present articles.

6. If the Commission is unable to obtain an agreement among the parties on a settlement of the dispute within six months of its initial meeting, it shall prepare as soon as possible a report of its proceedings and transmit it to the parties and to the depositary. The report shall include the

Commission's conclusions upon the facts and questions of law and the recommendations it has submitted to the parties in order to facilitate a settlement of the dispute. The six months time limit may be extended by decision of the Commission.

7. This Article is without prejudice to provisions concerning the settlement of disputes contained in international agreements in force between States.

Appendix II

PROPOSED CONVENTIONS

1. International Law Association Draft Single Convention
   on the Legal Control of International Terrorism (1980).

The Contracting States:

Considering that international terrorist offences constitute a common danger to the international community;

Considering that international terrorist offences violate
human rights as protected by international law;

Believing that this Convention will provide States with
an international standard for legal measures designed to
control and suppress international terrorist offences;

Have agreed as follows:

ARTICLE I: DEFINITION OF INTERNATIONAL TERRORIST OFFENCE.

1. An international terrorist offence is any serious act of
violence or threat thereof by an individual whether acting
alone or in association with other persons which is directed
against internationally protected persons, organizations,
places, transportation or communications systems or
against members of the general public for the purpose of
intimidating such persons, causing injury to or the death of
such persons, disrupting the activities of such international
organizations, of causing loss, detriment or damage to such
places or property, or of interfering with such transportation and communications systems in order to undermine
friendly relations among States or among the nationals of
different States or to extort concessions from States.

Conspiracy to commit, an attempt to commit, complicity
in the commission of, or public incitement to commit
offences as defined in the previous paragraph shall constitute an international terrorist offence.

199

2. For the purpose of the Convention:

(a) "Internationally protected persons" means those members of diplomatic, consular, or special missions, or of international organizations who have diplomatic or similar status, and foreign officials or persons invited to a state as official guests;

(b) "Internationally protected organizations" means an international intergovernmental organization or a non-governmental entity engaged in non-profit-making activities for the promotion of international understanding;

(c) "Internationally protected places" means

(i) premises of diplomatic, consular, or special missions and residences of the members of such missions;

(ii) premises of internationally protected organizations as defined in (b) above;

(iii) meeting places in use or scheduled to be used for an international conference, congress, convention, sports event, or other assembly;

(iv) buildings and facilities the destruction of which may endanger the public safety in one or more States;

(d) "Internationally protected transportation systems" means international land, air, and maritime transportation systems and buildings and facilities thereof;

(e) "Internationally protected communications systems" means postal services, submarine cables, telephone, radio, television, and satellite telecommunications systems in international use and any buildings and facilities thereof.

ARTICLE II: JURISDICTION

1. Each Contracting State undertakes to amend its present criminal law and procedure or to adopt new legislation comprehending the offence of international terrorism as defined in Article I and to make such offence punishable by a minimum sentence of two years' imprisonment.

2. Each Contracting State shall extend its jurisdiction to such an offence (a) committed within its territory, (b) committed by one or more of its nationals, or (c) committed within the territory of another Contracting State where the alleged offender has come into the territory of the first State.

3. Each Contracting State in whose territory an alleged offender is found shall without exception whatsoever either (a) submit the offender to its competent authorities for prosecution in accordance with its established criminal procedures or (b) return the offender by extradition or expulsion to another Contracting State which has requested his rendition in accordance with this Convention.

ARTICLE III: INTERNATIONAL RENDITION

1. An international terrorist offence as defined in this Convention shall be deemed to be an extraditable offence within the terms of any extradition treaty existing between or among the Contracting States or concluded by them in the future.

2. If a Contracting State which makes extradition conditional upon the existence of a treaty receives a request for extradition from another Contracting State with which it has no extradition treaty, it shall consider this Convention as the legal basis for extradition in respect of the offence.

3. Contracting States which do not make extradition conditional upon the existence of a treaty shall recognize

the offence as an extraditable offence between themselves.

4. Extradition shall be granted subject to the relevant procedural law of the requested State.

5. For the purpose of extradition, the offence shall be treated as if it had been committed not only in the place in which it occurred but also in the territory of each of the Contracting States in accordance with Article II (2).

6. An extradition request from the Contracting State in which the offence was committed shall have priority over other such requests if received by the Contracting State, in whose territory the alleged offender has been found, within thirty days after all Contracting States have been notified about the detention of the alleged offender.

7. An alleged offender may be returned to a requesting Contracting State by the process of expulsion provided that the offender shall have an opportunity to be heard and to be assisted by private or by publicly appointed counsel.

8. A person who is being held in jail for trial or who is serving a sentence in prison and who is released through terrorist extortion shall not be exempted thereby from extradition, expulsion, or criminal process, or from the obligation to complete his sentence.

9. An alleged offender may not invoke a political defence to rendition.

Article IV: Prosecution of Offenders

1. A Contracting State which takes custody of an alleged offender shall notify all other Contracting States without delay either directly or through the Secretary General of the United Nations.

2. A Contracting State shall submit the case of an alleged offender to its competent authorities for the purpose of prosecution within three months of taking custody of the offender.

3. The accused shall be accorded fair and humane treatment at all stages of the criminal proceedings. An accused who cannot afford counsel shall have access to publicly financed counsel.

4. The Contracting States shall provide one another the greatest measure of assistance in respect of the investigation and prosecution of a person charged with an international terrorist offence. This provision shall not affect obligations concerning the taking of testimony and mutual judicial assistance embodied in other conventions to which these States may be parties.

5. The statutory limitation for instituting prosecution for an international terrorist offence shall be ten years, except that where the offence has resulted in a death, there shall be no time limit.

6. Any person who has been tried in a Contracting State on a charge made in pursuance of this Convention and has been acquitted or, if convicted, has served a sentence therefor shall not be subject to further criminal proceedings on such charge.

7. An alleged offender may not invoke a political defence to the charge.

8. By agreement between the respective Contracting States and the offender, he may serve his sentence in his own State or in a different State from the prosecuting State.

ARTICLE V: RESPONSIBILITY OF CONTRACTING STATES

1. Each Contracting State shall, in pursuance of international and national law, take all practicable measures within its territory for the prevention of international terrorist offences as defined in Article I.

2. Each Contracting State shall co-operate with other Contracting States in the exchange of information or the

provision of administrative or judicial assistance looking to the prevention of international terrorist offences within their respective territories.

3. Any Contracting State which has failed to take measures to control an international terrorist offence as defined in Article I (a) by adopting legislation for the implementation of this Convention, (b) by co-operating with other Contracting States in the prevention of international terrorist offences within its territory, (c) by extraditing or expelling an alleged offender found within its territory, or (d) by submitting an alleged offender to its competent authorities for the purpose of prosecution shall be liable for the payment of damages for the death, bodily, or mental injury caused to any individual, whether a national or an alien, or for the loss, detriment or damage to real or personal property whether of national or alien ownership.

4. Liability for each victim shall be limited to proven damages not to exceed $100,000 (U.S.), exclusive of legal fees and costs. Liability for damage to or destruction of real or personal property shall be submitted to civil suit in the responsible State, or, by agreement of all parties, to arbitration.

5. A Contracting State which grants a haven to or otherwise co-operates with a person or persons accused of international terrorist offences in order to protect the lives of innocent persons is not exempted from the obligation under this Convention to extradite or expel such alleged offender or offenders, or to submit them to its authorities for the purpose of prosecution or from the obligation to pay damage to their victims.

ARTICLE VI: SETTLEMENT OF DISPUTES

1. A dispute between two or more of the Contracting States arising out of the interpretation or application of this Convention which cannot be settled by negotiation shall be submitted at the request of any party to the dispute to the International Court of Justice or to an arbitral tribunal.

2. The arbitral tribunal shall consist of three arbitrators. Each party to the dispute shall nominate one arbitrator. The third arbitrator shall be nominated by the President of the International Court of Justice. The arbitral tribunal shall establish its own procedure. The tribunal's award shall be by majority vote and shall be binding and final.

ARTICLE VII: RATIFICATION: ENTRY INTO FORCE: TERMINATION.

1. This Convention shall be open to ratification, acceptance, or approval. The appropriate instrument of commitment shall be deposited with the Secretary General of the United Nations.

2. The Convention shall enter into force three months after the date of deposit of the second instrument of ratification, acceptance, or approval.

3. The Convention may be denounced by written notification to the Secretary General of the United Nations. Such denunciation shall take effect twelve months after notification has been received by the Secretary General.

2. Procedural Aspects of International Law Institute Draft Convention on the Prevention and Punishment of Nuclear Theft and Violent Attacks Upon Nuclear Power Plants and Waste Storage Facilities (1976).

ARTICLE 1

The States Parties to the present Convention declare that the following acts are crimes of international significance:

(1) nuclear theft as defined in Article 2; and

(2) a violent attack upon a nuclear power plant or nuclear waste-storage facilities.

ARTICLE 2

For the purposes of the present Convention, the term "the crime of nuclear theft" shall mean the theft of nuclear material capable of being used either as an explosive device or for radiological contaminants in its original form or in any derivation of that form.

ARTICLE 3

Any person, irrespective of the motives involved, committing, participating in, directly inciting, abetting, encouraging or cooperating in the commission of (1) an act of the theft of nuclear material or (2) a violent attack upon a nuclear power plant or nuclear waste-storage facility commits an offence under this Convention.

ARTICLE 4

The Contracting Parties undertake to enact, in accordance with their respective Constitutions, the necessary legislation to make the offences set forth in Article 3 punishable by severe penalties.

206

ARTICLE 5

(1) Each State Party shall take such measures as may be necessary to establish its jurisdiction over the offences set forth in Article 3:

    (a) When the offence is committed in its territory; or

    (b) When the offence is committed by its national.

(2) Each State Party shall likewise take such measures as may be necessary to establish its jurisdiction over the offences set forth in Article 1 in the case where an alleged offender is present in its territory and the State does not extradite him to any of the States mentioned in paragraph 1 of this Article.

ARTICLE 6

The State Party in whose territory an alleged offender is found shall take appropriate measures to ensure his presence for prosecution or extradition.

ARTICLE 7

The Contracting Parties pledge themselves in such cases to grant extradition in accordance with their laws and treaties in force.

ARTICLE 8

The State Party in whose territory an alleged offender is present shall, if it does not extradite him, submit, without exception whatsoever and without undue delay, the case to its competent authorities for the purpose of prosecution, through proceedings in accordance with the laws of that State.

ARTICLE 9

(1) To the extent that the crimes set forth in Article 3 are not listed as extraditable offences in any extradition treaty existing between States Parties, they shall be deemed to be included as such therein. States Parties undertake to include those crimes as extraditable offences in every future extradition treaty to be concluded between them.

(2) If a State Party which makes extradition conditional on the existence of a treaty receives a request for extradition from another State Party with which it has no extradition treaty, it may, if it decides to extradite, consider this Convention as the legal basis for extradition in respect to those crimes. Extradition shall be subject to the procedural provisions and the other conditions of the law of the requested States.

ARTICLE 10

Any person regarding whom proceedings are being carried out in connection with any of the crimes set forth in Article 3 shall be guaranteed fair treatment at all stages of the proceedings.

ARTICLE 11

(1) States Parties shall afford one another the greatest measure of assistance in connection with criminal proceedings brought in respect of the crimes set forth in Article 3, including the supply of all evidence at their disposal necessary for the proceedings.

(2) The provisions of paragraph 1 of this Article shall not affect obligations concerning mutual judicial assistance embodied in any other treaty.

3. American Bar Association Model Convention on the Prevention and Punishment of Certain Serious Forms of Violence Jeopardizing Fundamental Rights and Freedoms (1980).

Recognizing the universally accepted principle that every human being has the right to life, liberty, and the security of his person,

Aware that acts violating this principle continue to occur throughout the Western hemisphere,

Wishing to take effective measures to ensure that perpetrators of such acts do not escape prosecution and punishment,

Convinced that extradition is an effective measure for achieving this result,

THE MEMBER STATES OF THE ORGANIZATION OF AMERICAN STATES HAVE AGREED UPON THE FOLLOWING ARTICLES:

Article 1

The following offenses shall come within the scope of this Convention:

a. an offense within the scope of the Convention for the Suppression of Unlawful Seizure of Aircraft, signed at the Hague on 16 December 1970;

b. an offense within the scope of the Convention for the Suppression of Unlawful Acts Against the Safety of Civil Aviation, signed at Montreal on 23 September 1971;

c. an offense within the scope of the Convention to Prevent and Punish the Acts of Terrorism Taking the Form of Crimes Against Persons and Related Extortion That Are of International Significance, signed at Washington on 2 February 1971;

209

d. an offense within the scope of the Convention on the Prevention and Punishment of Crimes Against Internationally Protected Persons Including Diplomatic Agents, signed at New York on 14 December 1973;

e. an offense within the scope of Article 11(e) of the Universal Postal Convention, signed at Tokyo on 14 November 1969;

f. an offense within the scope of the Genocide Convention adopted by the General Assembly of the United Nations on 9 December 1948;

g. an offense within the scope of Articles 13-16 of the Convention on the High Seas, signed at Geneva on 29 April 1958;

h. (1) the crime of "nuclear theft" which shall mean the theft of nuclear material capable of being used either as an explosive device or for radiological contaminants in its original form or in any derivation of that form. Any person or persons committing, participating in, directly inciting, encouraging or cooperating in the commission of the act of the theft of nuclear material shall be held accountable, irrespective of the motive involved;

(2) the crime of "nuclear sabotage" which shall mean a wilful act of violence against a nuclear facility in reckless disregard of the possible deleterious consequences or endangerment to the health of the neighboring communities. Any person or persons committing, participating in, directly inciting, encouraging or cooperating in the commission of the act of sabotage of a nuclear facility shall be held accountable, irrespective of the motive involved;

i. an offense within the scope of the United Nations General Assembly Declaration on the Protection of all Persons from Being Subjected to Torture and Other Cruel, Inhuman, or Degrading Treatment or Punishment of 9 December 1975 [Res. No. 3452 (XXX) 1];

210

j. an offense within the scope of the International Convention against the Taking of Hostages, signed at New York on 4 December 1979.

ARTICLE 2

Each Contracting State shall incorporate the offenses included in Article 1 into its domestic law and make the offenses punishable by severe penalties.

ARTICLE 3

1. Each of the offenses included in Article 1 shall be deemed to be included as extraditable offenses in any extradition treaty existing between Contracting States. Furthermore, Contracting States undertake to include such offenses as extraditable offenses in every extradition treaty to be concluded between them.

2. If a Contracting State that makes extradition conditional upon the existence of a treaty receives a request for extradition from another Contracting State with which it has no extradition treaty, it shall consider this Convention as the legal basis for extradition in respect of offenses included in Article 1. Extradition shall be subject to the procedural conditions provided for by the law of the requested State.

3. Contracting States that do not make extradition conditional upon the existence of a treaty shall recognize the offenses included in Article 1 as extraditable offenses between themselves subject to the procedural conditions provided for by the law of the requested State.

4. The offenses included in Article 1 shall be treated, for the purpose of extradition between Contracting States, as if they had been committed not only in the place in which they occurred but also in the territories of the Contracting States.

211

5. This Convention does not exclude any criminal jurisdiction exercised in accordance with domestic law.

ARTICLE 4

1. Contracting States shall afford one another the greatest measure of assistance in connection with criminal proceedings brought respecting offenses included in Article 1. The law of the State requested shall apply in all cases.

2. The provisions of paragraph 1 of this article shall not affect obligations under any other treaty, bilateral or multilateral, which governs or will govern, in whole or in part, mutual assistance in criminal matters.

ARTICLE 5

Nothing in this Convention shall be interpreted as imposing an obligation to extradite if the requested State has substantial grounds for believing that the request for extradition for an offense included in Article 1 has been made for the purpose of prosecuting or punishing a person on account of his race, religion, nationality or political opinion, or that that person's position may be prejudiced for any of these reasons.

ARTICLE 6

Nothing in this Convention shall be interpreted as imposing an obligation to extradite if the requested State has substantial grounds for believing that the request for extradition for an offense included in Article 1 has been made for the purpose of obstructing or preventing the prosecution or punishment of a person alleged to have committed an offense included within Article 1.

212

ARTICLE 7

Any person, who is in the custody of a Contracting State and who is suspected of committing an offense included in Article 1, is entitled to all the legal guarantees set forth in the American Declaration of the Rights and Duties of Man and in the American Convention on Human Rights.

ARTICLE 8

A Contracting State in whose territory a person suspected to have committed an offense included in Article 1 is found and which has received a request for extradition from a Contracting State shall, if it does not extradite that person, submit the case, without exception whatsoever and without undue delay, to its competent authorities for the purpose of prosecution. Those authorities shall make their decision in the same manner as in the case of any offense of a serious nature under the law of that State.

ARTICLE 9

Upon receipt of a request for extradition for an offense in Article 1, a Contracting State may refer the matter to the Inter-American Court of Human Rights pursuant to Article 64 of the American Convention on Human Rights for an advisory opinion as to whether granting the request for extradition would violate the provisions of this Convention. In like manner, a Contracting Party, which has made a request for extradition for an offense included in Article 1, may refer the matter to the Inter-American Court for an advisory opinion.

ARTICLE 10

Extradition shall not be granted for an offense included in Article 1 while a request for an Advisory Opinion from the Inter-American Court of Human Rights pursuant to Article 9 of this Convention is pending.

ARTICLE 11

The Contracting States urge the Inter-American Court of Human Rights to adopt procedures to ensure the expeditious handling of requests for advisory opinions pursuant to the provisions of this Convention.

ARTICLE 12

The provisions of all treaties and arrangements applicable between Contracting States are modified to the extent that they are incompatible with this Convention.

ARTICLE 13

This Convention shall remain open for signature by the Member States of the Organization of American States.

ARTICLE 14

This Convention shall be ratified by the signatory States in accordance with their respective constitutional procedures.

ARTICLE 15

The original instrument of this Convention, the English, French, Portuguese, and Spanish texts of which are equally authentic, shall be deposited in the General Secretariat of the Organization of American States, which shall send certified copies to the signatory Governments for purposes of ratification. The instruments of ratification shall be deposited in the General Secretariat of the Organization of American States, which shall notify the signatory Governments of such deposit.

ARTICLE 16

This Convention shall enter into force among the States that ratify it when they deposit their respective instruments of ratification.

ARTICLE 17

This Convention shall be subject to reservations only in conformity with the provisions of the Vienna Convention on the Law of Treaties signed 23 May 1969.

Reservations may not be entered in conjunction with Articles 7, 9 and 10.

ARTICLE 18

This Convention shall remain in force indefinitely, but any of the Contracting States may denounce it. The denunciation shall be transmitted to the General Secretariat of the Organization of American States, which shall notify the other Contracting States thereof. One year following the denunciation, the Convention shall cease to be in force for the denouncing State, but shall continue to be in force for the other Contracting States.

ARTICLE 19

This Convention ceases to have effect in respect to any Contracting State which withdraws from or ceases to be a member of the Organization of American States.

COUNTRY-BY-COUNTRY LIST OF RATIFICATIONS AND ACCESSIONS

Afghanistan
Tokyo Convention
Hague Convention
1949 Geneva Convention
U.P.U. Convention
Genocide Convention

Albania
1949 Geneva Convention
U.P.U. Convention
Genocide Convention
Convention on the Non-Applicability of Statutory Limitations

Algeria
1949 Geneva Convention
U.P.U. Convention
Genocide Convention
1951 Refugee Convention
1967 Refugee Protocol
O.A.U. Refugee Convention

Angola
U.P.U. Convention
1951 Refugee Convention

Argentina
Tokyo Convention
Hague Convention
Montreal Convention
1949 Geneva Convention
U.P.U. Convention

Genocide Convention
1933 Convention on Extradition
1951 Refugee Convention
1967 Refugee Protocol
1933 Convention on Political Asylum

Australia
Tokyo Convention
Hague Convention
Montreal Convention
New York Convention
1949 Geneva Convention
U.P.U. Convention
Genocide Convention
Commonwealth Extradition Scheme
1951 Refugee Convention
1967 Refugee Protocol

Austria
Tokyo Convention
Hague Convention
Montreal Convention
New York Convention
1949 Geneva Convention
U.P.U. Convention
Genocide Convention
European Convention on Terrorism
European Convention on Extradition
1951 Refugee Convention
1967 Refugee Protocol

Bahamas
Tokyo Convention
Hague Convention
Hostage Convention

1949 Geneva Convention
U.P.U. Convention
Genocide Convention

Bahrain
1949 Geneva Convention
U.P.U. Convention

Bangladesh
Tokyo Convention
Hague Convention
Montreal Convention
1949 Geneva Convention
U.P.U. Convention

Barbados
Tokyo Convention
Hague Convention
Montreal Convention
New York Convention
Hostage Convention
1949 Geneva Convention
U.P.U. Convention
Genocide Convention
Commonwealth Extradition Scheme

Belgium
Tokyo Convention
Hague Convention
Montreal Convention
1949 Geneva Convention
U.P.U. Convention
Genocide Convention
European Community's Agreement
Benelux Extradition Convention

1951 Refugee Convention
1967 Refugee Protocol

Benin
Hague Convention
1949 Geneva Convention
U.P.U. Convention
1951 Refugee Convention
1967 Refugee Protocol
O.A.U. Refugee Convention

Bhutan
Hostage Convention
U.P.U. Convention

Bolivia
Tokyo Convention
Hague Convention
Montreal Convention
1949 Geneva Convention
U.P.U. Convention
Bustamente Code
1951 Refugee Convention
1967 Refugee Protocol

Botswana
Tokyo Convention
Hague Convention
1949 Geneva Convention
U.P.U. Convention
Commonwealth Extradition Scheme
1951 Refugee Convention
1967 Refugee Protocol

Brazil
Tokyo Convention

Hague Convention
Montreal Convention
1949 Geneva Convention
U.P.U. Convention
Genocide Convention
Bustamente Code
1951 Refugee Convention
1967 Refugee Protocol
1928 Convention on Asylum
1933 Convention on Political Asylum
1954 Convention on Territorial Asylum
1954 Convention on Diplomatic Asylum

Bulgaria
Hague Convention
Montreal Convention
New York Convention
1949 Geneva Convention
U.P.U. Convention
Genocide Convention
Convention on the Non-Applicability of Statutory Limitations
Eastern European Bilateral Treaty Scheme

Burma
U.P.U. Convention
Genocide Convention

Burundi
Tokyo Convention
New York Convention
1949 Geneva Convention
U.P.U. Convention
1951 Refugee Convention
1967 Refugee Convention

Byelorussian S.S.R.
Hague Convention
Montreal Convention
New York Convention
1949 Geneva Convention
U.P.U. Convention
Genocide Convention
Convention on the Non-Applicability of Statutory Limitations
Eastern European Bilateral Treaty Scheme

Cameroon
Montreal Convention
1949 Geneva Convention
U.P.U. Convention
Convention on the Non-Applicability of Statutory Limitations
1951 Refugee Convention
1967 Refugee Protocol

Canada
Tokyo Convention
Hague Convention
Montreal Convention
New York Convention
1949 Geneva Convention
U.P.U. Convention
Genocide Convention
Commonwealth Extradition Scheme
1951 Refugee Convention
1967 Refugee Protocol

Cape Verde
Hague Convention
Montreal Convention

U.P.U. Convention

Central African Republic
1949 Geneva Convention
U.P.U. Convention
1951 Refugee Convention
1967 Refugee Protocol
O.A.U. Refugee Convention

Chad
Tokyo Convention
Hague Convention
Montreal Convention
1949 Geneva Convention
U.P.U. Convention
1951 Refugee Convention
1967 Refugee Protocol

Chile
Tokyo Convention
Hague Convention
Montreal Convention
New York Convention
Hostage Convention
1949 Geneva Convention
U.P.U. Convention
Genocide Convention
Bustamente Code
1933 Convention on Extradition
Inter-American Extradition Convention
1951 Refugee Convention
1967 Refugee Protocol
1933 Convention on Political Asylum

China, People's Republic of
Hague Convention
Montreal Convention
1949 Geneva Convention
U.P.U. Convention

China, Republic of
Tokyo Convention
Hague Convention
Montreal Convention
Genocide Convention

Colombia
Tokyo Convention
Hague Convention
Montreal Convention
1949 Geneva Convention
U.P.U. Convention
Genocide Convention
1933 Convention on Extradition
1951 Refugee Convention
1967 Refugee Protocol
1928 Convention on Asylum
1933 Convention on Political Asylum
1954 Convention on Territorial Asylum

Comoros
U.P.U. Convention

Congo
Tokyo Convention
1949 Geneva Convention
U.P.U. Convention
1951 Refugee Convention
1967 Refugee Protocol
O.A.U. Refugee Convention

Costa Rica
Tokyo Convention
Hague Convention
Montreal Convention
New York Convention
Convention on Crime Against Persons and Related
Extortion
1949 Geneva Convention
U.P.U. Convention
Genocide Convention
Treaty for Protection Against Anarchism
Bustamente Code
Inter-American Extradition Convention
1951 Refugee Convention
1967 Refugee Protocol
1928 Convention on Asylum
1933 Convention on Political Asylum
1954 Convention on Territorial Asylum
1954 Convention on Diplomatic Asylum

Cuba
1949 Geneva Convention
U.P.U. Convention
Genocide Convention
Convention on the Non-Applicability of Statutory Limitations
Bustamente Code
1928 Convention on Asylum
1933 Convention on Political Asylum

Cyprus
Tokyo Convention
Hague Convention
Montreal Convention
New York Convention

1949 Geneva Convention
U.P.U. Convention
European Convention on Terrorism
European Convention on Extradition
1975 Protocol to the European Convention on Extradition
Commonwealth Extradition Scheme
1951 Refugee Convention
1967 Refugee Protocol

Czechoslovakia
Hague Convention
Montreal Convention
New York Convention
1949 Geneva Convention
U.P.U. Convention
Genocide Convention
Convention on the Non-Applicability of Statutory Limitations
Eastern European Bilateral Treaty Scheme

Denmark
Tokyo Convention
Hague Convention
Montreal Convention
New York Convention
1949 Geneva Convention
U.P.U. Convention
Genocide Convention
European Convention on Terrorism
European Community's Agreement
European Convention on Extradition
1975 Protocol to the European Convention on Extradition
Nordic Extradition Scheme
1951 Refugee Convention

1967 Refugee Protocol

Djibouti
1949 Geneva Convention
U.P.U. Convention
1951 Refugee Convention
1967 Refugee Protocol

Dominica
1949 Geneva Convention

Dominican Republic
Tokyo Convention
Montreal Convention
New York Convention
Convention on Crime Against Persons and Related
    Extortion
1949 Geneva Convention
U.P.U. Convention
Inter-American Extradition Convention
Bustamente Code
1933 Convention on Extradition
1951 Refugee Convention
1967 Refugee Protocol
1928 Convention on Asylum
1954 Convention on Diplomatic Asylum

Ecuador
Tokyo Convention
Hague Convention
Montreal Convention
New York Convention
1949 Geneva Convention
U.P.U. Convention
Genocide Convention

Bustamente Code
Inter-American Extradition Convention
1933 Convention on Extradition
1951 Refugee Convention
1967 Refugee Protocol
1928 Convention on Asylum
1933 Convention on Political Asylum
1954 Convention on Territorial Asylum
1954 Convention on Diplomatic Asylum

Egypt
Tokyo Convention
Hague Convention
Montréal Convention
1949 Geneva Convention
U.P.U. Convention
Genocide Convention
Arab League Extradition Agreement
1951 Refugee Convention
1967 Refugee Protocol

El Salvador
Tokyo Convention
Hague Convention
Montreal Convention
New York Convention
Hostage Convention
1949 Geneva Convention
U.P.U. Convention
Genocide Convention
Treaty for Protection Against Anarchism
Bustamente Code
Inter-American Extradition Convention
1933 Convention on Extradition

1928 Convention on Asylum
1933 Convention on Political Asylum
1954 Convention on Territorial Asylum
1954 Convention on Diplomatic Asylum

Equatorial Guinea
U.P.U. Convention

Ethiopia
Tokyo Convention
Hague Convention
Montreal Convention
1949 Geneva Convention
U.P.U. Convention
Genocide Convention
1951 Refugee Convention
1967 Refugee Protocol
O.A.U. Refugee Convention

Fiji
Tokyo Convention
Hague Convention
Montreal Convention
New York Convention
U.P.U. Convention
Genocide Convention
Commonwealth Extradition Scheme
1951 Refugee Convention
1967 Refugee Protocol

Finland
Tokyo Convention
Hague Convention
Montreal Convention
U.N. Diplomatic Agents Convention

1949 Geneva Convention
U.P.U. Convention
Genocide Convention
European Convention on Extradition
Nordic Extradition Scheme
1951 Refugee Convention
1967 Refugee Protocol

France
Tokyo Convention
Hague Convention
Montreal Convention
1949 Geneva Convention
U.P.U. Convention
Genocide Convention
European Community's Agreement
1951 Refugee Convention
1967 Refugee Protocol

Gabon
Tokyo Convention
Hague Convention
Montreal Convention
1949 Geneva Convention
New York Convention
U.P.U. Convention
1951 Refugee Convention
1967 Refugee Protocol

Gambia
Tokyo Convention
Hague Convention
Montreal Convention
1949 Geneva Convention
U.P.U. Convention

Genocide Convention
Convention on the Non-Applicability of Statutory Limitations
Commonwealth Extradition Scheme
1951 Refugee Convention
1967 Refugee Protocol

German Democratic Republic
Hague Convention
Montreal Convention
New York Convention
1949 Geneva Convention
U.P.U. Convention
Genocide Convention
Convention on the Non-Applicability of Statutory Limitations
Convention on Protection of Nuclear Materials
Eastern European Bilateral Treaty Scheme

Germany, Federal Republic of
Tokyo Convention
Hague Convention
Montreal Convention
New York Convention
Hostage Convention
1949 Geneva Convention
U.P.U. Convention
Genocide Convention
European Convention on Terrorism
European Community's Agreement
European Convention on Extradition
1951 Refugee Convention
1967 Refugee Protocol

Ghana
Tokyo Convention
Hague Convention
Montreal Convention
New York Convention
1949 Geneva Convention
U.P.U. Convention
Genocide Convention
Commonwealth Extradition Scheme
1951 Refugee Convention
1967 Refugee Protocol

Greece
Tokyo Convention
Hague Convention
Montreal Convention
1949 Geneva Convention
U.P.U. Convention
Genocide Convention
European Convention on Extradition
1951 Refugee Convention
1967 Refugee Protocol

Grenada
Tokyo Convention
Hague Convention
Montreal Convention
1949 Geneva Convention
U.P.U. Convention

Guatemala
Tokyo Convention
Montreal Convention
1949 Geneva Convention
U.P.U. Convention
Genocide Convention

Treaty for the Protection Against Anarchism
Bustamente Code
Inter-American Extradition Convention
1933 Convention on Extradition
1928 Convention on Asylum
1933 Convention on Political Asylum

Guinea

U.P.U. Convention
Convention on the Non-Applicability of Statutory Limitations
1951 Refugee Convention
1967 Refugee Protocol
O.A.U. Refugee Convention

Guinea-Bissau

Hague Convention
Montreal Convention
1949 Geneva Convention
U.P.U. Convention
1951 Refugee Convention
1967 Refugee Protocol

Guyana

Tokyo Convention
Hague Convention
Montreal Convention
1949 Geneva Convention
U.P.U. Convention
Commonwealth Extradition Scheme

Haiti

New York Convention
1949 Geneva Convention
U.P.U. Convention

Genocide Convention
Bustamente Code
Inter-American Extradition Convention
1928 Convention on Asylum
1933 Convention on Political Asylum
1954 Convention on Territorial Asylum

Holy See
1949 Geneva Convention
U.P.U. Convention
1951 Refugee Convention
1967 Refugee Protocol

Honduras
Hostage Convention
1949 Geneva Convention
U.P.U. Convention
Genocide Convention
Bustamente Code
1933 Convention on Extradition
1933 Convention on Political Asylum

Hungary
Tokyo Convention
Hague Convention
Montreal Convention
New York Convention
1949 Geneva Convention
U.P.U. Convention
Genocide Convention
Convention on the Non-Applicability of Statutory Limi-
tations
Eastern European Bilateral Treaty Scheme

Iceland
Tokyo Convention
Hague Convention
Montreal Convention
New York Convention
Hostage Convention
1949 Geneva Convention
U.P.U. Convention
Genocide Convention
Nordic Extradition Scheme
1951 Refugee Convention
1967 Refugee Protocol

India
Tokyo Convention
New York Convention
1949 Geneva Convention
U.P.U. Convention
Genocide Convention
Convention on the Non-Applicability of Statutory Limitations
Commonwealth Extradition Scheme

Indonesia
Tokyo Convention
Hague Convention
Montreal Convention
1949 Geneva Convention
U.P.U. Convention

Iran
Tokyo Convention
Hague Convention
Montreal Convention
New York Convention
1949 Geneva Convention

U.P.U. Convention
Genocide Convention
1951 Refugee Convention
1967 Refugee Protocol

Iraq

Tokyo Convention
Hague Convention
Montreal Convention
New York Convention
1949 Geneva Convention
U.P.U. Convention
Genocide Convention

Ireland

Tokyo Convention
Hague Convention
Montreal Convention
1949 Geneva Convention
U.P.U. Convention
Genocide Convention
European Community's Agreement
European Convention on Extradition
1951 Refugee Convention
1967 Refugee Protocol

Israel

Tokyo Convention
Hague Convention
Montreal Convention
New York Convention
1949 Geneva Convention
U.P.U. Convention
Genocide Convention
European Convention on Extradition

1951 Refugee Convention
1967 Refugee Protocol

Italy

Tokyo Convention
Hague Convention
Montreal Convention
1949 Geneva Convention
U.P.U. Convention
Genocide Convention
European Community's Agreement
European Convention on Extradition
1951 Refugee Convention
1967 Refugee Protocol

Ivory Coast

Tokyo Convention
Hague Convention
Montreal Convention
1949 Geneva Convention
U.P.U. Convention
1951 Refugee Convention
1967 Refugee Protocol

Jamaica

New York Convention
1949 Geneva Convention
U.P.U. Convention
Genocide Convention
Commonwealth Extradition Scheme
1951 Refugee Convention
1967 Refugee Protocol

Japan

Tokyo Convention

Hague Convention
Montreal Convention
1949 Geneva Convention
U.P.U. Convention
1951 Refugee Convention
1967 Refugee Protocol

Jordan
Tokyo Convention
Hague Convention
Montreal Convention
1949 Geneva Convention
U.P.U. Convention
Genocide Convention
Arab League Extradition Agreement

Kampuchea, Democratic
1949 Geneva Convention
U.P.U. Convention
Genocide Convention

Kenya
Tokyo Convention
Hague Convention
Montreal Convention
1949 Geneva Convention
Hostage Convention
U.P.U. Convention
Convention on the Non-Applicability of Statutory Limi-
    tations
Commonwealth Extradition Scheme
1951 Refugee Convention
1967 Refugee Protocol

Korea, Democratic People's Republic of
Montreal Convention
1949 Geneva Convention
U.P.U. Convention

Korea, Republic of
Tokyo Convention
Hague Convention
Montreal Convention
1949 Geneva Convention
U.P.U. Convention
Genocide Convention

Kuwait
Tokyo Convention
Hague Convention
Montreal Convention
1949 Geneva Convention
U.P.U. Convention

Lao Republic
Tokyo Convention
1949 Geneva Convention
U.P.U. Convention
Genocide Convention

Lebanon
Tokyo Convention
Hague Convention
Montreal Convention
1949 Geneva Convention
U.P.U. Convention
Genocide Convention

Lesotho
Tokyo Convention
Hague Convention

Montreal Convention
Hostage Convention
1949 Geneva Convention
U.P.U. Convention
Genocide Convention
Commonwealth Extradition Scheme
1951 Refugee Convention
1967 Refugee Protocol

Liberia
Hague Convention
Montreal Convention
New York Convention
1949 Geneva Convention
U.P.U. Convention
Genocide Convention
1951 Refugee Convention
1967 Refugee Protocol
O.A.U. Refugee Convention

Libyan Arab Republic
Tokyo Convention
Hague Convention
Montreal Convention
1949 Geneva Convention
U.P.U. Convention

Liechtenstein
1949 Geneva Convention
U.P.U. Convention
European Convention on Terrorism
European Convention on Extradition
1951 Refugee Convention
1967 Refugee Protocol

Luxembourg
Tokyo Convention
Hague Convention
1949 Geneva Convention
U.P.U. Convention
Genocide Convention
European Community's Agreement
European Convention on Extradition
Benelux Extradition Convention
1951 Refugee Convention
1967 Refugee Protocol

Madagascar
Tokyo Convention
1949 Geneva Convention
U.P.U. Convention
1951 Refugee Convention

Malawi
Tokyo Convention
Hague Convention
Montreal Convention
New York Convention
1949 Geneva Convention
U.P.U. Convention
Commonwealth Extradition Scheme

Malaysia
1949 Geneva Convention
U.P.U. Convention
Commonwealth Extradition Scheme

Maldives
U.P.U. Convention

Mali

Tokyo Convention
Hague Convention
Montreal Convention
1949 Geneva Convention
U.P.U. Convention
Genocide Convention
1951 Refugee Convention
1967 Refugee Protocol

Malta

1949 Geneva Convention
Commonwealth Extradition Scheme
1951 Refugee Convention
1967 Refugee Protocol

Mauritania

Tokyo Convention
Hague Convention
Montreal Convention
1949 Geneva Convention
U.P.U. Convention
O.A.U. Refugee Convention

Mauritius

Hostage Convention
1949 Geneva Convention
U.P.U. Convention
Commonwealth Extradition Scheme

Mexico

Tokyo Convention
Hague Convention
Montreal Convention
New York Convention
Convention on Crime Against Persons and Related
Extortion

242

1949 Geneva Convention
U.P.U. Convention
Genocide Convention
O.A.S. Convention
Treaty for Protection Against Anarchism
1933 Convention on Extradition
1928 Convention on Asylum
1933 Convention on Political Asylum
1954 Convention Territorial Asylum
1954 Convention on Diplomatic Asylum

Monaco
1949 Geneva Convention
U.P.U. Convention
Genocide Convention
1951 Refugee Convention

Mongolia
Hague Convention
Montreal Convention
New York Convention
1949 Geneva Convention
U.P.U. Convention
Genocide Convention
Convention on the Non-Applicability of Statutory Limitations

Morocco
Tokyo Convention
Hague Convention
Montreal Convention
1949 Geneva Convention
U.P.U. Convention
Genocide Convention
1951 Refugee Convention

1967 Refugee Protocol
O.A.U. Refugee Convention

Mozambique
U.P.U. Convention

Nauru
U.P.U. Convention

Nepal
Tokyo Convention
Hague Convention
Montreal Convention
1949 Geneva Convention
U.P.U. Convention
Genocide Convention

Netherlands
Tokyo Convention
Hague Convention
Montreal Convention
1949 Geneva Convention
U.P.U. Convention
Genocide Convention
European Community's Agreement
European Convention on Extradition
Benelux Extradition Convention
1951 Refugee Convention
1967 Refugee Protocol

New Zealand
Tokyo Convention
Hague Convention
Montreal Convention
1949 Geneva Convention
U.P.U. Convention

Commonwealth Extradition Scheme
1951 Refugee Convention
1967 Refugee Protocol

Nicaragua

Tokyo Convention
Hague Convention
Montreal Convention
New York Convention
Convention on Crime Against Persons and Related
  Extortion
1949 Geneva Convention
U.P.U. Convention
Genocide Convention
Bustamente Code
1933 Convention on Extradition
Inter-American Extradition Convention
Central American Extradition Convention
1951 Refugee Convention
1967 Refugee Protocol
1928 Convention on Asylum
1933 Convention on Political Asylum

Niger

Tokyo Convention
Hague Convention
Montreal Convention
1949 Geneva Convention
U.P.U. Convention
1951 Refugee Convention
1967 Refugee Protocol
O.A.U. Refugee Convention

Nigeria

Tokyo Convention

Hague Convention
Montreal Convention
1949 Geneva Convention
U.P.U. Convention
Convention on the Non-Applicability of Statutory Limitations
Commonwealth Extradition Scheme
1951 Refugee Convention
1967 Refugee Protocol

Norway
Tokyo Convention
Hague Convention
Montreal Convention
New York Convention
Hostage Convention
1949 Geneva Convention
U.P.U. Convention
Genocide Convention
European Convention on Terrorism
European Convention on Extradition
Nordic Extradition Scheme
1951 Refugee Convention
1967 Refugee Protocol

Oman
Tokyo Convention
Hague Convention
Montreal Convention
1949 Geneva Convention
U.P.U. Convention

Pakistan
Tokyo Convention
Hague Convention

Montreal Convention
New York Convention
1949 Geneva Convention
U.P.U. Convention
Genocide Convention
Commonwealth Extradition Scheme

Panama
Tokyo Convention
Hague Convention
Montreal Convention
New York Convention
1949 Geneva Convention
U.P.U. Convention
Genocide Convention
Bustamente Code
Inter-American Extradition Convention
1933 Convention on Extradition
1951 Refugee Convention
1967 Refugee Protocol
1928 Convention on Asylum
1933 Convention on Political Asylum
1954 Convention on Territorial Asylum
1954 Convention on Diplomatic Asylum

Papua New Guinea
Tokyo Convention
Hague Convention
Montreal Convention
1949 Geneva Convention
U.P.U. Convention
Genocide Convention

Paraguay
Tokyo Convention

Hague Convention
Montreal Convention
New York Convention
1949 Geneva Convention
U.P.U. Convention
1951 Refugee Convention
1967 Refugee Protocol
1928 Convention on Asylum
1933 Convention on Political Asylum
1939 Treaty on Political Asylum
1954 Convention on Territorial Asylum
1954 Convention on Diplomatic Asylum

Peru
Tokyo Convention
Hague Convention
Montreal Convention
New York Convention
1949 Geneva Convention
U.P.U. Convention
Genocide Convention
Bustamente Code
1951 Refugee Convention
1928 Convention on Asylum
1933 Convention on Political Asylum
1939 Treaty on Political Asylum
1954 Convention on Diplomatic Asylum

Philippines
Tokyo Convention
Hague Convention
Montreal Convention
New York Convention
1949 Geneva Convention

U.P.U. Convention
Genocide Convention
Convention on the Non-Applicability of Statutory Limitations
Convention on the Protection of Nuclear Materials
1951 Refugee Convention
1967 Refugee Protocol

Poland

Tokyo Convention
Hague Convention
Montreal Convention
1949 Geneva Convention
U.P.U. Convention
Genocide Convention
Convention on the Non-Applicability of Statutory Limi-
tations
Eastern European Bilateral Treaty Scheme

Portugal

Tokyo Convention
Hague Convention
Montreal Convention
1949 Geneva Convention
U.P.U. Convention
European Convention on Extradition
1951 Refugee Convention
1967 Refugee Protocol

Qatar

Hague Convention
Montreal Convention
1949 Geneva Convention
U.P.U. Convention

Romania
Tokyo Convention
Hague Convention
Montreal Convention
New York Convention
1949 Geneva Convention
U.P.U. Convention
Genocide Convention
Convention for the Non-Applicability of Statutory Limitations
Eastern European Bilateral Treaty Scheme

Rwanda
Tokyo Convention
New York Convention
1949 Geneva Convention
U.P.U. Convention
Genocide Convention
Convention on the Non-Applicability of Statutory Limitations
1951 Refugee Convention
1967 Refugee Protocol

Saint Lucia
1949 Geneva Convention
U.P.U. Convention

Saint Vincent and the Grenadines
1949 Geneva Convention
U.P.U. Convention
Genocide Convention
Convention on the Non-Applicability of Statutory Limitations

San Marino
1949 Geneva Convention
U.P.U. Convention

Sao Tome and Principe
1949 Geneva Convention
U.P.U. Convention
1951 Refugee Convention
1967 Refugee Protocol

Saudi Arabia
Tokyo Convention
Hague Convention
Montreal Convention
1949 Geneva Convention
U.P.U. Convention
Genocide Convention
Arab League Extradition Agreement

Senegal
Tokyo Convention
Hague Convention
Montreal Convention
1949 Geneva Convention
U.P.U. Convention
1951 Refugee Convention
1967 Refugee Protocol
O.A.U. Refugee Convention

Seychelles
Tokyo Convention
Hague Convention
Montreal Convention
New York Convention
1949 Geneva Convention
U.P.U. Convention

1951 Refugee Convention
1967 Refugee Protocol

Sierra Leone
Tokyo Convention
Hague Convention
Montreal Convention
1949 Geneva Convention
U.P.U. Convention
Commonwealth Extradition Scheme
1951 Refugee Convention
1967 Refugee Convention

Singapore
Tokyo Convention
Hague Convention
Montreal Convention
1949 Geneva Convention
U.P.U. Convention
Commonwealth Extradition Scheme

Solomon Islands
1949 Geneva Convention

Somalia
1949 Geneva Convention
U.P.U. Convention
1951 Refugee Convention
1967 Refugee Protocol

South Africa
Tokyo Convention
Hague Convention
Montreal Convention
1949 Geneva Convention
U.P.U. Convention (expelled 11 June 1981)

Spain
Tokyo Convention
Hague Convention
Montreal Convention
1949 Geneva Convention
U.P.U. Convention
Genocide Convention
1951 Refugee Convention
1967 Refugee Protocol

Sri Lanka
Tokyo Convention
Hague Convention
Montreal Convention
1949 Geneva Convention
U.P.U. Convention
Genocide Convention
Commonwealth Extradition Scheme

Sudan
Hague Convention
Montreal Convention
1949 Geneva Convention
U.P.U. Convention
1951 Refugee Convention
1967 Refugee Protocol
O.A.U. Refugee Convention

Surinam
Tokyo Convention
Hague Convention
Montreal Convention
1949 Geneva Convention
Hostage Convention
U.P.U. Convention

1967 Refugee Protocol

Swaziland
1949 Geneva Convention
U.P.U. Convention
Commonwealth Extradition Scheme
1967 Refugee Protocol

Sweden
Tokyo Convention
Hague Convention
Montreal Convention
New York Convention
Hostage Convention
1949 Geneva Convention
U.P.U. Convention
Genocide Convention
European Convention on Extradition
1975 Protocol to the European Convention on Extradition
1978 Second Protocol to the European Convention on Extradition
Nordic Extradition Scheme
1951 Refugee Convention
1967 Refugee Protocol

Switzerland
Tokyo Convention
Hague Convention
Montreal Convention
1949 Geneva Convention
U.P.U. Convention
European Convention on Extradition
1951 Refugee Convention
1967 Refugee Protocol

Syrian Arab Republic
Tokyo Convention
Hague Convention
Montreal Convention
1949 Geneva Convention
U.P.U. Convention
Genocide Convention

Tanzania, United Republic of
1949 Geneva Convention
U.P.U. Convention
Commonwealth Extradition Scheme
1951 Refugee Convention
1967 Refugee Convention

Thailand
Tokyo Convention
Hague Convention
Montreal Convention
1949 Geneva Convention
U.P.U. Convention

Togo
Tokyo Convention
Hague Convention
Montreal Convention
New York Convention
1949 Geneva Convention
U.P.U. Convention
1951 Refugee Convention
1967 Refugee Protocol
O.A.U. Refugee Convention

Tonga
Hague Convention

Montreal Convention
1949 Geneva Convention
U.P.U. Convention
Genocide Convention
Commonwealth Extradition Scheme

Trinidad and Tobago
Tokyo Convention
Hague Convention
Montreal Convention
New York Convention
Hostage Convention
1949 Geneva Convention
U.P.U. Convention
Commonwealth Extradition Scheme

Tunisia
Tokyo Convention
Hague Convention
Montreal Convention
New York Convention
1949 Geneva Convention
U.P.U. Convention
Genocide Convention
Convention on the Non-Applicability of Statutory Limitations
1951 Refugee Convention
1967 Refugee Protocol

Tuvalu
1949 Geneva Convention
U.P.U. Convention

Turkey
Tokyo Convention

Hague Convention
Montreal Convention
New York Convention
1979 Geneva Convention
U.P.U. Convention
Genocide Convention
European Convention on Extradition
1951 Refugee Convention
1967 Refugee Protocol

Uganda
Hague Convention
1949 Geneva Convention
U.P.U. Convention
Commonwealth Extradition Scheme
1951 Refugee Convention
1967 Refugee Protocol

Ukrainian S.S.R.
Hague Convention
Montreal Convention
New York Convention
1949 Geneva Convention
U.P.U. Convention
Genocide Convention
Convention on the Non-Applicability of Statutory Limitations
Eastern European Bilateral Treaty Scheme

U.S.S.R.
Hague Convention
Montreal Convention
New York Convention
1949 Geneva Convention
U.P.U. Convention

Genocide Convention
Conventions on the Non-Applicability of Statutory Limitations
Eastern European Bilateral Treaty Scheme

United Arab Emirates
Tokyo Convention
Hague Convention
Montreal Convention
1949 Geneva Convention
U.P.U. Convention

United Kingdom
Tokyo Convention
Hague Convention
Montreal Convention
New York Convention
European Convention on Terrorism
1949 Geneva Convention
U.P.U. Convention
Genocide Convention
European Community's Agreement
Commonwealth Extradition Scheme
1951 Refugee Convention
1967 Refugee Protocol

United States
Tokyo Convention
Hague Convention
Montreal Convention
New York Convention
Convention on Crime Against Persons and Related Extortion
1949 Geneva Convention
U.P.U. Convention

1933 Convention on Extradition
1967 Refugee Protocol

Upper Volta
Tokyo Convention
1949 Geneva Convention
U.P.U. Convention
Genocide Convention
1951 Refugee Convention
1967 Refugee Protocol

Uruguay
Tokyo Convention
Hague Convention
Montreal Convention
New York Convention
Convention on Crime Against Persons and Related
  Extortion
1949 Geneva Convention
U.P.U. Convention
Genocide Convention
Inter-American Extradition Convention
1951 Refugee Convention
1967 Refugee Protocol
1928 Convention on Asylum
1939 Treaty on Political Asylum
1954 Convention on Territorial Asylum
1954 Convention on Diplomatic Asylum

Venezuela
Convention on Crime Against Persons and Related
  Extortion
1949 Geneva Convention
U.P.U. Convention
Genocide Convention
Bustamente Code

Inter-American Extradition Convention
1954 Convention on Territorial Asylum
1954 Convention on Diplomatic Asylum

Vietnam
Tokyo Convention
Hague Convention
Montreal Convention
1949 Geneva Convention
U.P.U. Convention
Genocide Convention

Western Samoa
Commonwealth Extradition Scheme

Yemen, Arab Republic of
1949 Geneva Convention
U.P.U. Convention
1967 Refugee Protocol

Yemen, Democratic
1949 Geneva Convention
U.P.U. Convention
1951 Refugee Convention
1967 Refugee Protocol

Yugoslavia
Tokyo Convention
Hague Convention
Montreal Convention
New York Convention
1949 Geneva Convention
U.P.U. Convention
Genocide Convention
Convention on the Non-Applicability of Statutory Limitations

Eastern European Bilateral Treaty Scheme
1951 Refugee Convention
1967 Refugee Protocol

Zaire

Tokyo Convention
Hague Convention
Montreal Convention
New York Convention
1949 Geneva Convention
U.P.U. Convention
Genocide Convention
1951 Refugee Convention
1967 Refugee Protocol
O.A.U. Refugee Convention

Zambia

Tokyo Convention
1949 Geneva Convention
U.P.U. Convention
Commonwealth Extradition Scheme
1951 Refugee Convention
1967 Refugee Protocol
O.A.U. Refugee Convention

Zimbabwe

1951 Refugee Convention
1967 Refugee Protocol

Index

A

263

E

S

U

UGANDA.
Ratifications and Accessions, p. 257.

UKRAINIAN S.S.R.
Ratifications and Accessions, p. 257.

UNITED ARAB EMIRATES.
Ratifications and Accessions, p. 258.

UNITED KINGDOM.
Ratifications and Accessions, p. 258.

UNITED STATES.
Ratifications and Accessions, p. 258.

UPPER VOLTA.
Ratifications and Accessions, p. 259.

URUGUAY.
Ratifications and Accessions, p. 259.

U.S.S.R.
Ratifications and Accessions, p. 257.

V

VENEZUELA.
Ratifications and Accessions, p. 259.

VESSELS.
Hijackers.
Bilateral treaty, p. 157.

VIETNAM.
Ratifications and Accessions, p. 260.

W

WAR.
Geneva Convention for Protection of Civilian Persons in Time of War, p. 101.

WAR CRIMES.
Convention on the Nonapplicability of Statutory Limitations to War Crimes, p. 118.

WESTERN SAMOA.
Ratifications and Accessions, p. 260.

Y

YEMEN, ARAB REPUBLIC OF.
Ratifications and Accessions, p. 260.

YEMEN, DEMOCRATIC.
Ratifications and Accessions, p. 260.

YUGOSLAVIA.
Ratifications and Accessions, p. 260.

Z

ZAIRE.
Ratifications and Accessions, p. 261.

ZAMBIA.
Ratifications and Accessions, p. 261.

ZIMBABWE.
Ratifications and Accessions, p. 261.

2751